ASK your INVISIBLE ASPECTS

ISBN: 1-4537-1675-0
ISBN-13: 9781453716755

ASK your INVISIBLE ASPECTS

ASPECTS

How to DEPROGRAM You

Bonnie Baumgartner

Table Of Contents

I have written about programming in my books:
Integrate yourself, Programming INFANTS and
Sexual Energy

My website is **www.mysticknowing.com**
Free on line dictionary is available
Free book can be downloaded

Acknowledgments

I am grateful to the COUNCIL of TEACHERS who are volunteers from the human and angelic educators helping us move to higher levels of compassion on both sides of the veil. Teachers LEARN by teaching and teach by LISTENING.

My gratitude goes to all those with and without biology that have trusted my listening skills. Thank you to all the HUMANS that have helped me with their creativity, consciousness, and time.

Svali Speaks http://www.mindcontrolforums.com/svali_speaks.htm

The Illuminati Formula Used to Create an Undetectable Total Mind Controlled Slave by Cisco Wheeler and Fritz Springmeier 1995

Dan Laudicina who gives a different point of perception and fills in awareness that I miss.

Becky Beebe who sees pictures, slide shows and stories to add clarity to the many changes happening in the now moment

Sarah Hyatt that has clear communication with her invisible aspects and a slightly different take on our illusion here on earth.

Torben Hansen that shares personal knowledge and balance. Torben sees repetitive patterns to evolve out of.

http://www.look4insight.com
http://awarenesshealsme.com

Kelly Arbogast knows things. He created and serves as the Webmaster on the Mystic Knowing website. http://www.mysticknowing.com

Introduction

Key to illuminati programming is that the slave never has conscious awareness or control of what they do. They do have the "illusion of deciding" what they want to do.

Close to a third of the earth's population were CO-VERTLY raised to be "compliant illuminati mind-controlled slaves" designed to help bring in the New World Order and New World Religion. The slave being conscious would get in the way of the illuminati's smooth running dark and perverse operation, which they are VERY proud of. The illuminati consider humans a lower, less evolved form of life to be used anyway they want to use us and we have allowed that.

To break your illuminati programming or any other programming you were subjected to as a helpless infant or child work with "your invisible aspects" and follow the universal laws.

Your invisible aspects are mostly parts of yourself you can't see generally because they vibrate differently than humans. They can and do make their presence know through our sensory perceptions and have saved your biology and sanity many, many times before. The human essence is 10% of the 90% invisible aspects or conglomerate. Other energies come and go, as we need them. Our 90%ers leave clues and gifts to help the human build its spiritual wisdom. Our invisible aspects may be light and some shades of gray. The human MUST DISCERN what is coming from their light bits and what is coming from their darker bits.The human is RE-SPONSIBLE for educating their darker aspects and support-ing them to lighter ways of reasoning. "The New Age" said we could send the dark away or WALL them off and that is not true. We function in a free will zone and are responsible for ALL OUR aspects. To make consistently LIGHT choices and align with universal law you will need to be very alert at first until you get the hang of it.

The illuminati were first to inhabit earth and created the various religions on roughly the same theme. ALL the religions tell the same stories we find in the bible and other religious texts. The stories are all rewrites of your basic "Sa-tan" from Draco or "EL" from Saturn that are designed to glorify and empower the little human or reptilian. They all carry the same message of "follow this deity" or be punished or be killed or you will not be saved. This VERY common religious theme is a very low and dark vibration of control, force and manipulation.

All the religions claim to be doing "gods work" by go-ing through the universe dominating and assimilating inferior creatures like humans are said to be. Our earth religions encourage GUILT, control and FORCING our "version of god," on the "native" or "pagan" humans while taking their land, natural resources and financial assets. I do not see any difference from what the reptilians do in the universe and what humans do here on earth. All the "dark gods" take your free will and ability to choose and THINK for your self. They keep you fearful with "fire and brimstone," or focused with "sound and light shows" to keep your attention diverted outside the self and keep your "VEHICLE" or biology alive and amused to prevent you from seeing the larger picture of what is really true.

Our essence is infinite our vehicle or biology dying is not such a big deal. Our vehicle has died MANY times before while our essence remains as it was. Our soul can go darker with many small negative choices and vampirism the human may choose. The little human can get "drunk with the power of their vehicle" and "little human gods." This can be a VERY sad dark story.

THAT is NOT the way of it in higher vibrations.

When YOU have diverted YOU and your awareness with distractions from your inner alignment with your invisible aspects, universal law and the legion of light your invisible aspects can't channel universal energy to you. Without that energy the vehicle or biology starts to die unless you can siphon light energy from others that carry light. In fact that is exactly what the dark gods and the illuminati are doing all the time siphoning light from humans. When dark ones feed on each other and there is no energy left to siphon, the biology and essence or soul start disintegrating into basic elements and become space dust. This can take a long time and many others may go dark and die in the process.

Yes, 74% of the earth's population is unconscious and not carrying much light if any and they siphon energy all the time from anyone that allows it. The universal laws are clear on how to deal with that much darkness.

Do NOT upset yourself about it.

Do NOT organize to fight it or try to change it. They have free will "just like you do" to raise their vibration and lift themselves out at anytime they wish. They have made that choice until they decide differently.

Bring up your vibration and light to evolve OUT of the low vibration.

The Universal Law of **ALLOWING** means dropping ALL judgment, blame and emotional attachment to what others DO, SAY or think. They are on their own spiritual path with their invisible aspects. Allowing requires granting others, even children the right to BE just as they are, doing whatever THEY choose. With higher vibrational thought, truths and self-love we evolve out of the circle of darkness, force, manipulation and control. TOLERANCE is not allowing it is holding negative thoughts that will affect you.

Our invisible aspects are trying to "awaken" and raise the vibration of their humans asking for direction and answers. On a planet of free will, the human must ASK for the information and support that will heal them. Your awareness of what is TRUE will heal you.

The Illuminati forces the two year old to carry alters for Druidism, Christianity and Satanism. When the illuminati slave places their faith in a "human or reptilian" created faith or belief systems they "WAIT to be SAVED." Waiting to be saved means you have not awakened to the legion of light and universal law that says you must save YOUR SELF.

The Universal Law of **PERPETUAL TRANSMUTATION of ENERGY** is that all humans have the power to change the conditions in their lives. Raising your vibration IS HARD work. You need to stay in your biology and focus your thoughts. We ALL have the skill set to do that. What you have attracted you have to UNDO yourself. Humans can and many have, raised their vibration out of the low dark vibration of the illuminati and / or very dark families.

I know people that talk about mind control and being programmed give out warnings about having their programming triggered or restimulated. After working with many illuminati slaves, my thought on the subject is GOOD, let us trigger your programming so you can have conscious awareness of what you do and take control of it. YOU decide what is best for you. Be in charge of what you do by staying in present time all the time. Working with your invisible aspects and alignment WITH the universal laws will raise your vibration. 74% of the earth's population are unconscious or dissociated so someone or something else controls them. Their choice was to allow that control. You can consciously DECIDE to crash or overrule your own programming by BEING AWARE OF IT. You are only a slave and nothing more when you live your life being triggered all the time. When you accomplish things for the cult you are supporting darkness, perversion and control. Is that what you want to do with your FREE WILL on this planet?

The Universal Law of **FREE WILL** is divine will granting each entity the right to DIRECT and PURSUE his or her life so long as he or she does not violate the same right of others. A right that excludes the rights of others is NOT DIVINE. There is nothing divine about the illuminati OR abusive families and clans.

No one is going to rescue you. A 100% dark person can "go light" step by step if they choose to. Ask your invisible aspects your percent of light. Ask for a slide show of what you need to do to go lighter?

Going against the universal laws creates suffering to strongly point out a better direction for you. IGNORANCE or disregard of universal law invites serious censure and doubt from your invisible aspects. The higher angelic realms do not judge breaking human law or "reptilian programming," they patiently wait for you to see the light and start communing with them. All living things with awareness and knowledge of the laws have the VITALITY and STRENGTH to gather what they need to grow and develop out of their dark confusion. The inner character you have shows in your growth or DECAY that develops during your challenging struggles with matter, darkness and duality.

External results of an action are not significant. In our physical world of lower vibration on earth, THINGS and THOUGHTS are temporary. Working within the laws of the universe you are assured of positive outcomes eventually.

Understand that everything in the universe is energy including humans and their programs or stuck behavior patterns. ASK your invisible aspects to give you a slide show to increase your awareness of how your suffering keeps darkness strong and well feed.

UNIVERSAL ENERGY or COSMIC FLOW or INTELLIGENCE is the base energy that permeates all life in the universe or cosmos and is infinite. This is unconditional love energy with NO agenda or attachments. It has the highest vibration there is and flows a sense of wellbeing, compassion and knowingness through our invisible aspects or 90%er, this is not dark or the devil or evil.

Chapter 1
HOW to DEPROGRAM

To dissociate is to disconnect, to abandon or go away.

This ability to disconnect is highly prized by predators and programmers and anyone that wants to FORCE another to do something they would NEVER do on their own. When they give you a choice it is always a TRICK offering one thing and giving another, they drug and traumatize.

Victims that are too small, weak or emotionally terrorized want to go away because they do not WANT to know what is going to happen next. They feel powerless to do anything about what will be happening to their biology that is trapped by a predator. In one respect victim and predator are in agreement. The victim withdraws their consciousness and control to the predator or programmer that takes over and controls the outcomes. When you are an infant and child disconnection helps you stay alive one more day through one more assault on your biology and your psyche. This pattern that was developed in childhood follows you into your adult life WITHOUT you ever questioning YOUR practice of disconnecting from your awareness and sensory perceptions.

When your awareness or essence goes away so does your investment with you and what happens to you goes away! When your awareness is gone so is your RESPONSIBILITY to yourself gone.

The universal law of PERPETUAL TRANSMUTATION of ENERGY is that all humans have the power to change the conditions in their lives. Raising your vibration IS HARD work.

You NEED TO STAY in your biology to raise your vibration.

You need to FOCUS your thoughts to raise your vibration.

What you have attracted you have to UNDO yourself but probably not with a child's biology, but generally speaking the ADULT needs to. If you want to deprogram your childhood traumas or illuminati "TRAINING" and release the EMOTIONAL charge of "training" or abuse it is ALWAYS best to move to the earliest INCIDENT on the chain of that particular type of event.

People that are recovering memories that indicate they have been programmed by the illuminati or molested often by grandpa FREQUENTLY do not go back far enough in childhood or concurrent lifetimes to release the emotional charge. When the emotional pain isn't released the human lives in the pain body or past time. They are always reexperiencing the pain when there is nothing-painful happening in present time. Going back to the earliest incident and "owning it" takes the emotional charge off of it and releases the emotion charge on all the times after the first time that particular thing happened.

When you have been "trained" or programmed by the illuminati you can also KNOW that your programming was started when you were a fetus or right after birth. This earliest programming laid in is what CREATES the dysfunctional adult that cannot function well in the greater society. The adult that is very stressed with a hair trigger and has eyes like a "deer in headlights" is suffering from their earliest programs carefully crafted for the infant to NEVER ALLOW that child and adult to think for it self or know what it does. That individual is always in fear and obedience to "the family" and what they want. They have seen that the punishment can include death.

Infants raised in cults tend to be EMOTIONALLY arrested at age 2 or 3 years in adulthood because of their training NEVER to think for them self. The cult does not want their members THINKING just act as you are told. One who thinks or feels or is BONDED emotionally to another human or thing is much harder to control and force. Being bonded to another might cause your programming to crash. Having an accident or feelings might start crashing your programming or old hidden memories might show up in your awareness. The kinds of memories you have are so strange you know you are going crazy.

All programming done later in life is BUILT on the initial programming all the children get around the world. AND that would be close to a third of the population. Understanding those BASIC programs laid down and the DAMAGE they do to an infants thought, psychic and emotions is the explanation for the adult's inability to function in our society and ALL their emotional handicaps. They frequently can't hold down a job for long and are sexual addicts because that IS PART of their training. They generally have relationships with other programmed individuals so their "intimate interactions" are triggering each other's programs. More likely one "handles" the other. There is no real intimacy because the CORE PERSONALITY seldom makes an appearance. If you want an honest interaction you have to get the core personality to show up. That is no easy task. Even a programmed individual interacting with their child is programmed with the "baby talk program" and the child will go through all the programming the parent had.

Prisoners in jail, abusive spouses, prostitutes, abused and programmed people generally have no compassion for them self or others. They are self absorbed like all dysfunctional children and adults are BECAUSE they have no awareness of their abuse as an infant and as a young child they have NO COMPASSION for them self. For what that child endured. Without compassion for YOUR ABUSE you repeat the cycle until you see or know what REALLY happened. That is why people marry the same type of spouse and have the same type of friends. To hopefully see the abusive pattern they are STUCK in.

Until you see your pattern of behavior there is the compulsion to repeat.

When the individual becomes aware of their abuse and sensory perceptions of the events the compassion for the self and healing starts to happen. Compassion for the abused infant and child brings the core personality out to take control of your biology and the integration of your split off aspects designed to COPE with each new assault on the core personality. That is exactly WHY the predator wants to keep you dissociated. Left on your own you might start integration of your alters and get a lot harder to control and force.

The ritually abused need to reconnect to the childhood sensory experiences they had. They DO NOT need to know each incident. Their invisible aspects can give them slide shows of events and or the FEELINGS they experienced as children of what was TRUE. No more pretty, FAKE story cover-ups and lies. Deceptions only help the predator or programmer.

ASK just ask out loud for your invisible aspects to give you the feelings or pictures. One way or another they will get them to you. Just because family members can't remember this information or are unable to relay it doesn't mean its not there. To have an effective deprogramming you MUST go back to the first 2 years they are the MOST traumatic to the human. The child feels things a 100 times stronger than the adult would that had the same experience. Working with your invisible aspects will give you the information you need. You need to be brave enough to stay in your biology and in present time.

◑◐

Daytime ABANDONMENT Programming

After birth the trauma starts with DAYTIME ABAN-DONMENT programming, which starts at birth and never really stops. This programming is for ALL the cult children. Those not in the cult that have dissociated caretakers experience the same traumas to some degree.

The infant's environment itself BECOMES programming. No matter how the infant behaves it is IGNORED and ABUSED physically and emotionally in the daytime. Nurturing and caretaking by the parent or cult happens at NIGHT-TIME only. The time for cult activities is what is important and that is the night.

As any psychologist will tell you it is TRAUMATIC for the infant to not have their basic needs met and ignored. This leads to core personality splits because the infant goes into red alert first and then despairs into apathy. They feel invisible, abandoned and hopeless. No chance to develop self loves there. The child is forced to deal with adults that are INCONSISTENT, UNRELIABLE and abusive. The adults have multiple personalities or Dissociative Identity Disorder, DID and act robotically. There is no one home to interact with.

Ask your invisible aspects, out loud, if you had daytime abandonmentprogramming? Get a yes or no. Ask for a slide show or feeling show so you can know how you really felt as an infant.

WOODPECKER GRIDS are and were located in airplane hangers on military bases, which have been able to house thousands of tiny cages just large enough for human babies. In grids of 1,000 to 3,000 were babies from ceiling to floor and the cages were HOT WIRED, electrified on the ceiling, bottom and sides so the BABIES locked inside could receive horrific electric shocks to traumatize them to split the core personality for illuminati needs and control. Do you need to ask someone else if that traumatizes the child?

Sometimes a baby rolled up in a fetal position and gave up their will to live.

The child saw a flash of light when high direct current voltage was applied. Later this flash of light was used with hypnosis to let them think they slipped into another dimension. In the Peter Pan program it is RIDING the LIGHT. After endured the Woodpecker Grid Cages for days the infant is BRUTALLY raped. Naval Ordinance test station / NOTS was their first torture. The California INSTITUTE of Technology at Pasadena is intimately connected to China Lake's research and the Illuminati. Most of their work is for the intelligence agencies, not the military. They developed red / green color programming there.

A MARBLE SLAB served as an altar where black-hooded robed people would take a bone-handled knife and sacrifice little children in front of the other children in the cages. Charles Manson was a programmed Monarch slave and received his initial "training" or programming at China Lake. His cult was 45 miles northwest of China Lake at the remote Myers and Barker ranches.

Ask your invisible aspects, out loud, if you had experienced woodpecker grids? Get a yes or no. If you get a yes ask for a slide show or feeling show.

A list of major programming centers with each site's programming specialties is kept. Infants are brought into base by trains, planes and cars. The lumber mill had an agreement to secretly house the children who had their mouths tapped. Neighbors in the area were bought off and warned that if they talked they would be in trouble for broaching national security. Tied into this network was a Catholic Monastery between Sheridan and McMinnville, close to the rail network. The Union Train Station in Portland, Oregon has underground tunnels where children were temporarily warehoused in cages before continuing on their journey. The Jesuits were active in this part of the child procurement. Catholic adoption agencies, pregnant nuns, third world parents, and parents who will sell their children were sources of children for programming. Procuring batches of 1,000 or 2,000 children is no problem for the Illuminati working through intelligence agencies such as the CIA, NIS, DIA, FBI, and FEMA.

Possibly you didn't get born into the illuminati but got "jumped in" after birth because you didn't say no.

If you managed to live through all of that you get to the STEPS of DISCIPLINE Programming. The illuminati start this program and training at 20—24 months. And NO they do not remember these experiences most of the time because there is always a trigger to make them forget.

STEPS of DISCIPLINE Programming

STEPS of DISCIPLINE Programming or training the illuminati start at 20—24 months with all the children. It is easy and fast dissociation and mind numbingly traumatic splintering them into more alters, dissociation and unconscious loyalty to the cult.

1st **NOT to NEED** the toddler is placed in a training room without any sensory stimulus with gray, white, or beige walls and left alone for hours or all day. If the child begs the adult to stay or screams the child is beaten and told the periods of isolation will increase until they learn to stop being WEAK. The child is often found rocking or hugging itself in a corner occasionally CATATONIC from fear.

The trainer RESCUES the child giving food, drink and bonding becoming also the savior of the child. Trainer tells the child "the family" told them to rescue him or her because they love the child. That leaves a 2-year-old child panicked, confused and unable to think and reinforces dependency.

Ask your invisible aspects, out loud, if you have been trained not to need? Get a yes or no. Ask for a slide show or feeling show.

2nd **NOT to WANT** is done similar to "not to need." In the next few years that get reinforced with an adult entering the room with a large pitcher of ice water and food. If the child asks for either as the adult is eating or drinking in front of the child he or she is SEVERLY punished for being WEAK and NEEDY. The child continues to not notice the needs of their biology. This stops sensory awareness and feelings.

Ask your invisible aspects, out loud, if you have been trained not to want? Get a yes or no. Ask for a slide show or feeling show.

3rd **NOT to WISH** the child is placed in a room with favorite toys or objects. A KIND adult comes into the room and plays with the child. They engage in fantasy play about the child's secret WISHES or DREAMS so trust is slowly gained. LATER the child is severely punished for any aspect of wishing or fantasy shared with the adult and the destruction of the child's favorite toys or ANY illusion of safety the child has left. This step is repeated with variations often. The child believes the illuminati reads their thoughts and feelings.

These irrational lies are not challenged because the young child has a variety of alters that take turns dealing with the different experiences. One alter bounds with the trainer. A different alter tells the wishes and dreams. Another alter takes the electric shock and another takes the punishment. No one alter is aware of ALL that has happened. Let alone what it means. The core personality hides out. The alters NEVER have a complete picture. The child functions with the reptilian brain of survival so there are no higher thought processes going on.

Ask your invisible aspects, out loud, if you have been trained not to wish? Get a yes or no, if yes. Ask for a slide show or feeling show.

4th is **SURVIVAL of the FITTEST** and starts at age 2 to create perpetrator alters in the child. ALL cult members are expected to be perpetrators. Two children around the same age and a trainer are together. One child is severely beaten for long periods of time by the trainer and then that child is told to hit the other child watching or they will be beaten further. If the child refuses it is punished severely. The child watching is punished too and told to punish the first child. If the child continues to refuse or cries or tries to hit the trainer instead they continue to be beaten. This is repeated until the child finally complies and beats the other child. Both children are to consider this as NORMAL healthy moral behavior.

Ask your invisible aspects, out loud, if you have been trained in survival of the fittest? Get a yes or no. Ask for a slide show or feeling show.

5th **CODE of SILENCE** starts at 2 years using many different strategies as a child becomes more verbal and after a ritual or group gathering. The child is asked about what they saw or heard during the meeting. They tell the trainer what they saw and get severely beaten or TORTURED creating new ALTERS. The child is to guard the memories of what was seen on pain of death. Setups and role-play like this go on and on. Can you see why an illuminati raised child might not have any memories or not want to remember any of this nuttiness.

Ask your invisible aspects, out loud, if you have been trained in the code of silence? Get a yes or no, when yes. Ask for a slide show or feeling show.

6th **BETRAYAL and TWINNING** starts in infancy and is formalized at ages 6-7 continuing into adulthood. Betrayal is an important dark SPIRITUAL principle. The child is placed in situations where an adult who is kindly rescues the child and gains its trust several times. After months to a year of bonding with the child, he or she will turn to the adult for help. The adult backs away MOCKING the child and abusing it.

Ask your invisible aspects, out loud, if you have been trained to betray? Get a yes or no. Ask for a slide show or feeling show.

TWINNING "set ups" create twin bonds in children that are NOT twins. The child is allowed to play with and become close to another child in the cult from earliest child-hood. At some point early on the child is told that the other child is actually their "twin" and they were separated at birth. It is a great SECRET and they can't tell. Cult children are very lonely and isolated and continue to be that way in adulthood. They are overjoyed to have a friend to do things with.

Later they will be FORCED to hurt each other. If one "twin" is considered expendable it will die at its twins hand or be forced to watch the other die. Both twins will be forced to disclose their secrets to a trainer or cult leader. If one twin refuses to kill, hit or hurt the other they will be brutal-ized by the trainer and the refusing twin is told that the child was hurt because of their refusal to comply. This devastates both children. This goes against all the training the society at large gives a child.

Ask your invisible aspects, if you have been twinned? Get a yes or no, if yes. Ask for a slide show or feeling show.

The child's emotional, social and physical needs and de-velopment are ignored and turned against the child by the cult and the parent and "the religion" to TRAIN and ritually abuse the child to be compliant and not think. The adult child has learned to surrender to the control of their cult by dissociating, mentally and emotionally abandoning their biology in service to the cult. The training is so thorough that the illuminati slave REFUSES to take responsibility for his or her own biology. The ritually abused do not feel their biology or mind even belongs to them. Deep down they feel someone else is responsible for integrating them and none of it is really their concern.

Children raised in satanic cults are dysfunctional adults most of the time because they were never allowed to move through the developmental stages most children experience. They were never allowed to function in this reality. Their reality is controlled and manipulated all the time to the needs or wants of the illuminati. They run like well oiled robots in constant fear of more suffering.

Marilyn Monroe and Michael Jackson were illuminati sex slaves and we all saw how well they handled reality. Neither was enjoying their earth experience and both died without and clarity about what happened to them. Neither remembered their childhood, the first few years. The beatings Michael remembered were "focus changes" from the horrible traumas before being beaten.

Owning what you really feel gives you the power to release and replace the belief's your childhood experiences created in you. That way you can increase your self-worth, self-love and release your self-sabotage, victimhood and develop the bigger picture and a healthier auric field. Not knowing your own vibration means you also might not know when you have chosen and invited in lower vibrations or had them invited in by your "family" the illuminati so your job by default is to invite the darkness OUT of you and your life.

Consciously or unconsciously you have done the inviting and also need to do the uninviting, ushering out of what is keeping your vibration low through entrainment and your minute by minute choices.

The universal LAW of ENTRAINMENT REQUIRES that two resonances or vibrations existing in the same location MUST adjust and combine to have a single resonance. For Example, on a scale of 1-10 if one individual is at 3 and the other is at a 7 the law of entrainment requires that they will both be at 5 ish.

The other possibility is when one resonance is overpowering it will pull the other to their level so you both would move to 3,4 or 6,7. Every thought we have creates energetic ripples. Our body anchors our energetic layers, which fan out in every direction in ever-widening circles of vibrating frequency at six feet from the biology. PRINCIPLE of Reconciliation and / or entrainment allows different qualities to get unified into similarities to diminish differences and decrease conflict and promote commonalities and oneness. Playing with darkness helps you go dark.

ALPHA Programming

ALPHA Programmingis the easiest brain wave to reach and includes the youngest and easiest alters to reach. Infants and children live in alpha states and need "training" to enter other brain waves for long periods to serve the illuminati agenda. There are systems of alters and access codes. Different alternate personalities in the child service adults sexually and are often placed in alpha programming and may be coded as RED in some systems.

ALPHA is considered the FOUNDATION for all other programs to control the mind. Trainers program in how to TORTURE, use **espionage**, develop photographic memory and VISUAL ACUITY.

Ask your invisible aspects, out loud, if you have alpha programming installed or any programming similar to that? Get a yes or no, when it is yes. Ask for a slide show or feeling show.

BASIC ILLUMINATI PROGRAMMINGis based upon Illuminati and Nazi goals to create a Master race in part through GENETICS and mostly through FORCE. Mind-controlled slaves will be given multifunctional programming and usually are used to help program other slaves. Parents program children. These children will often receive lavish experiences as well as talks to convince them that they are part of the ELITE. Maybe they aren't, the lies to manipulate are endless.

By 4 years of age the child's weaknesses and strengths are charted and the child's destiny in life is determined. The chart has the occupation the child will be created for and their function in the overall Illuminati plan. Their programs are determined and the appropriate alters get created. The map of the Land of Oz in the Wizard of Oz books was frequently used for the front parts or alters of a system built as a city of entities having unity and multiplicity.

Ask your invisible aspects do I have any Illuminati programming, yes or no?

Ask your invisible aspects do I have any programming? Who installed it? Can you please give me a slide show of pictures and or feelings?

BETA Programmingis coded blue and builton Alpha programming in infants and children. BETA is the 2nd easiest brain wave to reach and associated with aggression, survival and SEXUAL impulses. Beta holds cult PROTECTORS, internal warriors and MILITARY systems. All cult families go on military retreats and camps a few times a year to keep all members ready for the military TAKE over of the civilian population when the "One World Order" takes control.

Beta sex slaves are programmed to have charm, seductive skills, charisma, and creativity. Beauty is in the eye of the beholder, and the programmers can put almost any kind of body to use as a sex slave in the crime syndicate pornographic movies or Internet porn of horrible atrocities like having one's head chopped off while having sex or aborting a fetus. Beta alters are used as the Black Widow for espionage and blackmail.

Early sexual abuse events will be used or created to anchor this programming. Beta altars generally see themselves as cats. The SCORPIAN vibration was government programmed into the Monarch sex slaves both male and female. The BETA model can have sex ONLY with whom his or her master allows her to have sex with and they CANNOT refuse sexually servicing someone. Slaves are consistently belittled and compared unfavorably to others. The children are also available for movers and shakers to sexually use around the world at parties and possible for blackmail.

Ask your invisible aspects do I have beta programming?

Ask your invisible aspects do I have any sexual programming from my first few years of life? Who installed it? Can you please give me a slide show of pictures and or feelings?

BRAIN STARVATION programming is done by severely limiting SUGAR and PROTIEN in take. Water deprivation taught to parents who raise slaves is used to raise the brain's TEMPERATURE, which happens when the brain swells from lack of water. The brain gets woozy and overheated and hallucinates then the slave can't remember clearly what awful things they see or experience. Water deprivation combined with electroshock makes it harder yet for the victim to remember anything.

Heavy exercise along with long periods of little sleep (2-3 hours/day) causes an overproduction of endorphins and victims begin to robotically respond to commands. Under this stress the brain may flip functioning from right to left and vice-versa.

Ask your invisible aspects have I been brain starved any my first few years of life? Can you please give me a slide show of pictures and or feelings? What were you to forget?

Are you developing compassion for yourself as a small YET?

Lower vibrating entities find it easy to play their games without resistance from higher vibrations because higher vibrations follow the universal law of allowing.

LAW of ALLOWING means dropping ALL judgment, blame and emotional attachment to what others DO, SAY or think. They are on their own spiritual path with their invisible aspects. Allowing requires granting others, even children the right to BE just as they are doing whatever THEY choose with the adult protecting and supporting them. With higher vibrational thought, truths and self-love we evolve out of the circle of darkness, force and control. TOLERANCE is not allowing it is holding negative thoughts.

The legion of light ARE light-beings that are primarily consciousness and formless and not in a place as they exist in a quantum state everywhere. They do not judge or force anything or anyone they emanate unconditional love and are the Intelligence behind all creation, whether we acknowledged it or not. The little human fascination of PERSONAL creation is self-exploration as opposed to the legion of light creation for the good of all. Discern legion of light from religious endeavors of humans.

Why are we getting programmed?

Dark needs sustenance and a source of energy all the time to sustain itself.

The reptilians believe they are doing "gods work" by going through the universe dominating and assimilating inferior creatures like humans and making them slaves and a food source and energy source.

Their god is a large white winged dragon with icy blue eyes that MUST be obeyed. The god of humans sounds a lot like that, bearded white boy with white tunic that preaches love and stop thinking for yourself and do what I tell you, a milder version of the Draco god that wants to own us physically. Human gods want to own our mind and behavior physically and energetically.

"The Christians" or "missionaries" on earth save "heathens or pagans" to please their god. They grab land and make money. Americans did that to the American Indians.

Acts of compassion and freedom, I think not, acts of control and force in "gods' name. If the reptilians are our genetic parent and handlers we have grown up just like them.

Neither god wants to "set the human free" to work with their invisible aspects to create in the universe.

PRINCIPLE ofFREEDOM is to give space for expansion and growth for ALL without restricting others freedom and space to grow. Universal law frees each and everyone. No one is free until each is free and all are freeing each other.

LAW of DIVINE MANIFESTATION is win-win-win-win to benefit all involved and harm done to none. Any harm to another in the process or outcome of manifestation is not DIVINE and carries karmic debt. Many are piling up their karmic debt.

Chapter 2
COLOR CODES

A simple system to organize codes for nonreaders like most 2 year-olds are is using **COLOR Programming** or CODING that will be used for the rest of their life unless they CONSCIOUSLY choose to leave this control system they were forced into by dissociated mind controlled parents.

As always training starts with DRUGING through food, drink or injection, the child is hypnotized and TRAUMA-TIZED. They strap the NAKED 2 year old down on the cold metal table. All done before the "training" gets underway. The training is done over and over again to lay in each and every traumatized alter and there is endless reinforcing of trauma and drugging.

For example training to be the color blue.

The child is put into a room of neutral color like white or beige. The trainer will dress in all blue and there will be blue lighting and blue objects in the room. The 2 year old child will awaken from the abuse still in a trance and is told that blue is GOOD and blue will PROTECT them from harm and blue people don't get HURT. The trainer calls up a young child alter or core split from the child's internal system of alters and tells the child they will learn how to BECOME blue. The child is asked if it wants to be blue. That way the child has the illusion of choice and culpability, the child feels responsible for what happens to them.

All children feel responsible for what happens to them. When they are abused the child thinks it has been BAD and deserves what is happening to them. They blame them self and the trainer assures them in deed and word that it is their fault. That installs a lifetime of feeling GUILTY and not worthy. How cool is that!

If the 2 year old says yes, it wants to be BLUE like the trainer they continue on.

If the child says no it is re-traumatized until it says yes.

The naked child is told it cannot wear clothing until it EARNS the right to wear beautiful blue clothes. They are forced to act in blue ways. The training to "be blue" is done many times. Any time in the future they want to access the child's blue system and put "blue alters" to work the trainer will "trigger them" or call them up with the blue color or wear a piece of clothing in the color they want to call up.

Or on television the blue-faced men or blue popsicles will trigger their blue programming and strengthen it or that alter will be called out to DO or KNOW something.

ASK your invisible aspects if around 2 years of age was I strapped down to a metal table, yes or no?

ASK your invisible aspects do I have blue programming yes or no? Ask for a slide show or feeling show so you can know how you really felt about being programmed for blue as a toddler.

ASK am I afraid to say "NO" yes or no? If yes ask for a slide show or feeling show so you can reexperience what emotional trauma you had when you said NO. Ask for a show of the "no's" on your chain. Some might go to past lifetimes or the future accept and own that if it does.

Beta programming is often color coded blue and is associated with aggression. The beta state often holds cult protectors, internal warriors, sexual aggression, sex slaves and military systems. All cult family's members including small children go on military retreats or camps a few times a year to keep all members ready for the military TAKE over of the civilian population when the "New World Order" and "New World Religion" take control of earth.

ASK do I have illuminati military programming, yes or no?

For those not traumatized in this formal of a system, a color may have been something you focused on or associate with abuse of one type or another so ask your invisible aspects if you have an "emotional charge" to release associated with a particular color yes or no? Ask for a slide show.

Many people have color codes and don't realize it. They see or view a certain color THROUGH a particular alters eyes. Sometimes their alter is in a certain colored room or wear only certain colored clothes or one eye sees red and the other eye sees green if they are red / green programmed.

Each alter is programmed on how IT SHOULD view life, THINK, act and function in their job. The job done right EVERY time is what is important in programming. This programming would be linked to an internal computer. The programmers have the perfect ways to make the slave controlled. The slave MONITORS it self and then will tell on itself when it has NOT done things right. This is why deprogramming a slave by reproducing the original programs does not work well. Understanding all the why's and how things are done is exceedingly time consuming and there are too many traps to circumvent. Earth is in a higher vibration now and you can consciously DECIDE to crash your own programming by

BEING AWARE OF IT consciously, and not letting it control you. KNOW you are only a slave and nothing more when you live your life being triggered all the time. When you accomplish things for the cult you are SUPPORTING darkness, perversion and control is that what you want to do with your FREE WILL on this planet of contrast?

Universal Law of **FREE WILL** is divine will granting each entity the right to DIRECT and PURSUE his or her life so long as he or she does not violate the same right of others. A right that excludes the rights of others is NOT DIVINE.

No one is going to rescue you.

Universal Law of **PERPETUAL TRANSMUTATION of ENERGY** is that all humans have the power to change the conditions in their lives. Raising your vibration IS HARD work. You need to stay in your biology. Focus your thoughts. We ALL have the skill set to do that. What you have attracted you have to UNDO yourself. You are very culpable!

The illuminati can only reach and manipulate the little human or any entity that has a low vibration and a low percentage of light. When you have 80% light or more and are working with and communing with your higher self or soul you are above the level the illuminati can reach and manipulate. A 100% dark person can go light step by step if they choose to that.

Ask your invisible aspects your percent of light. Ask what you need to do next to go lighter. Ask your invisible aspects if they will help and support you?

COLORS

COLOR CODES are found in a standard 13 x 13 x 13 = 2,197 possible alternate personalities or alters or splits in the Illuminati alter system and they are coded with 13 different colors. Each computer inside the SLAVE was given a color. Color-coding within the Illuminati Mind Control system is fairly consistent. The hierarchy of colors in a system is often as follows from the top down Platinum, Gold, Silver, Purple, Black, Red, Green, Brown, White, Orange, Yellow and Pink. Each color has different meanings and RANK.

Joseph Mengala and his programmers used a large doll-house with 26 rooms. Each room was painted one of the 13 different colors for the child to visualize. 13 front and the 13 back computers or rooms were in the dollhouse. While electro shocking the child, to change their focus a different colored scarf would come out and be shown to the child to build colored ribbons or rooms internally. The alters would be dehumanized one step further into thinking they were ribbons. Ribbon programming represented their location, who they are and what they protect.

The color tells you what your job is and who inside of the alters is a friend and who is not. There are some "light alters" to balance out all of the "dark alters." When an internal or external handler wants you to do something, they know which color group of alters to call out. Like the blue will do military moves. Color programming is one of the first programs to be done or laid in. The same system is done the same way around the world. That way any cult member or trainer around the world can activate your programming and get CONSISTENT results from YOU the programmed slave without free will because you are programmed and you are following it. Programming is interchangeable and accessible around the universe when you are locked into being a person that LIVES to AVOID getting hurt anymore.

SUFFERING

Going against the universal laws creates suffering to strongly point out a better direction. Your IGNORANCE or disregard of universal law invites serious censure and doubt from your invisible aspects. The higher angelic realms does not judge breaking human law or reptilian programming, they patiently wait for you to see the light and start communing with them.

All living things with awareness and knowledge of the laws have the VITALITY and STRENGTH to gather what they need to grow and develop out of their dark confusion. The inner character you have shows in your growth or DE-CAY that develops during your challenging struggles with matter, darkness and duality.External results of an action are not significant. In our physical world of lower vibration on earth, THINGS and THOUGHTS are temporary. Working within the laws of the universe you are assured of positive outcomes eventually. Understand that everything in the universe is energy including humans and their programs or stuck behavior patterns.

ASK your invisible aspects to give you a slide show to increase your awareness of how your suffering keeps darkness strong and well feed. Programming and forcing are against the universal law of allowing.

The universal law of **ALLOWING** means dropping ALL judgment, blame and emotional attachment to what others DO, SAY or think. They are on their own spiritual path with their invisible aspects. Allowing requires granting others, even children the right to BE just as they are doing whatever THEY choose. With higher vibrational thought, truths and self-love we evolve out of the circle of darkness, force and control. TOLERANCE is not allowing it is holding negative thoughts.

Programming, controlling and forcing are only present in the low dark vibrations of duality. Your AWARENESS of your dark patterns and your willingness to heal will put you in the **VOID** or with a feeling of EMPTINESS that is a portal from what is USUAL and customary for YOU to an empty aloneness. A void happens after there is an OUTWARD expansion of energy and you realize a belief you always operated with is NOT true at a higher vibration and you need to release it. You are in the void or space between releasing old and adopting new truths.

When old beliefs and truths crumble there is a great deal of grieving, HURT, pain and JOY that can be experienced during this process. Grieve the changes and any lose you might have. Cut cords to relationships no longer serving you. Give back any darkness you have carried for others as a child and especially from family members. Something new will come into your awareness. There is MENTAL and EMO-TIONAL processing and transmuting go on in you. Generally voids last a few months or weeks.

Ask your invisible aspects if you are in a void yes or no? What old beliefs are you releasing?

Sections of alters in the brain have specific jobs and are color-coded.

Parts of the computers inside your brain and mental body are also color-coded.

In the colors presented below I have mixed up the alter sections and computers to convey the intricacy and insidiousness of the programming. Each level gained is built on more suffering and torture, drugging and hypnosis to feed the illuminati agenda of having skilled obedient slaves that do not think for them self.

CLEAR is a secret or SHELL alter to DECEIVE the outside world. These are alters that serve as images or a stage for other alters including "Guardian of the Vail." Clear is used for secret areas. Internal programmers or handlers can switch colors to protect the programming. Protecting the slave is not so important. Clear can take on any color and that is dangerous because anyone can step in and take control.

ASK your invisible aspects if there is anything the core personality needs to see or feel about the color clear?

PLATINUM is the ultimate. NO ONE is more superior than platinum alters. Platinum alters remain hidden until you find them and beware if you do. You must die before you can see the Seven Seals the platinum hides and protects. Not all of the "Illuminated ones" reach the level of Platinum. This power and control must be earned generationally through your bloodlines and DNA.

ASK your invisible aspects the percent of reptilian DNA you have?

SILVER alters are satanic ones who perform high level Satanic rituals and that includes the "Mothers of dark." They are the spiritual bodies that know the paranormal. They can astral project and communicate with other people's silver alters.

ASK your invisible aspects do I have paranormal skills? Are they controlled and used by the illuminati? Are my skills present for me to connect and commune with my invisible aspects?

GOLD is in control when platinum isn't. Gold talks mainly to purples. Gold internal alters are mainly organizers, administrators, judges and generally the boss. Gold is the perfectionists because if everything isn't done perfectly there will be great torture and suffering for the slave. The All Seeing Eye is here in gold. The shutter of the All-seeing eye of the computer is a "child alter" that opens and shuts the eye. It knows what goes on in all of the system subconsciously but if it discovered by a therapist or other intruder the eye shuts and the human slave cannot talk. They are at top of the pyramid unless they decide to flip it. Gold is the color for the supreme leadership in the system and the "Grand Druid Council."

ASK your invisible aspects how many lifetimes you were born into the illuminati? ASK your invisible aspects your souls purpose for being born into the cult family this lifetime?

PURPLE altars' or handlers are the INTERNAL ABUSERS in the system. They watch and are in control and invisible to the other colors. Purple feels superior. They are the mafia connection, the drug dealers, and the politicians. They fail to believe the torture they have suffered to get to the purple level because they are programmed to deny it. They are the Illuminated ones and only take orders from the gold council. One alter in the purple level is on the Gold Council and purple gives the "gold orders" throughout the system.

NO ONE or alter REALIZES they have been given an order, especially NOT the slave. The appropriate alter is called out and does what it was told to do. When the human "DECIDES" or an alter is ordered to MOVE, change jobs, "falls in love" have a child, get MARRIED, meet someone, go someplace or call a number the slave has done what they were ordered to do. When they do not do what they were ordered to do they tell on them self and another order goes out. The human has the ILLUSION it was their choice and it has NEVER been their choice, an internal and external handler controlled all they have ever done.

Purple tells the BIOLOGY when it needs to be punished, cut or die. They deserve it and that won't hurt purple if the biology dies. ANOTHER one of the many irrational lies the trainer installs in the illuminati slave. The slave is not capable of questioning what they are not conscious of. The Illuminati teaches their slaves to forget abuse and reframe it in their mind as "training."

When you have not been formally traumatized by the illuminati and your family severely abused you in their own personal way. Know that your abusers also told you many lies but you can generally remember what the abuser said and hopefully clear up the confusion and lies they gave you to serve their purpose.

ASK your invisible aspects about the lie you believe that causes you the most trouble at this time. Ask for a slide show.

VIOLET-PURPLE alters are front alters placed to make the slave appear "normal and cute" to deceive the public and the triggered slave. Small CHILD alters are placed into boxes. There is "baby talk programs" going back and forth between the children and adult that says nothing but appear to be intimate and loving. There is also adult-to-adult baby talk.

ASK your invisible aspects if you fail to care for your biology because of programming laid in as a child yes or no?

ASK your invisible aspects if you ignore your biology because you think it betrayed you yes or no? Can you get a slide show of the earliest incident?

BLACK reads and memorizes details about the Illuminati locally and nationally.

They perform many of the VERY many cult rituals. Do what Satan wants or you will FEEL the pain instead of SENDING it on down to the other color alters. Black does NOT feel unless they are the one being PUNISHED. Black is born out of the satanic "moonchild ritual" to demonize the fetus. High-level demons and family demons are placed in fetuses in Moonchild rituals. Blood sacrifices and human sacrifices are ALWAYS required for this level of magic.

Black takes orders from the purple.

The Delta and Beta alters are coded black and do the DIRTY work for the cult like blackmail and assassination. Delta Teams are part of the CIA's psychic warfare programming. The army has an occult fighting force that practices witchcraft with its warfare or psychic operations and this includes Satanists officers.

Black "Nexus alters" are the alters that connect to other colored alters, they are connecting links or groups that go between various system parts.

RED are the alters that get raped and sexually abused. The black alters lied and tricked red by telling them red was superior and in control. Red altars see themselves as witches and having the power of witchcraft and believe they have great spiritual power. They DENY their abuse. RED are sexual arousal alters.

Ask your invisible aspects about red triggers or programs you have like being sexually seductive that get you in trouble in the "normal world"?

BROWN is disguises or chameleon-like. A "hidden system" and may hold CIA programming and high level governmental programming or in the beta system they are the courier, operations, learning to tail a subject, or "drop a tag" depending on the trainer.

GREEN is where access by family or "illuminati" members takes place for those loyal to their cult families. They get most of the cult pain and abuse that happens at home like being raped daily from birth on by your father to "train you" boys and girls are "trained" the same way. Mom physically and sexually tormenting the female infant because she "took the husband away from her." The craziness never stops. They are cat alters recognizing they have been abused BUT deny their abuse to "protect the illuminati family" and their many abusers.

In what world does any of that make sense? That is why the world at large cannot grasp the evil pervasiveness of the illuminati and what it has done always on earth. They brought these behaviors, their religion and training from Draco and covertly passed it on to trusting humans. The only way to stop it is for you to do it individually and by your self, communing with your invisible aspects and aligning YOUR behavior with universal law now!

LIGHT GREEN are god and goddess alters formed in triads that function in the Illuminati ceremonies and rituals.

EMERALD GREEN or dark green are Satan alters or the Anti-Christ alters and are considered the most sacred occult color.

EMERALD CITY LIBRARY is that some alters in the illuminati system only function as photographic memories and store pages and pages of information including the codes of the their entire internal system. The libraries contain the historical genealogies of satanic DNA from early ancient times like Atlantis to the present.

EMERALD TABLETS of THOTH from 36,000 years ago written by Thoth, anAtlantean Priest-King that also founded a colony in Egypt. The ancient tablets describe the arrival of the Anunnaki their ability to SHAPE SHIFT and possess people in power because they didn't carry much light. The tablets were written by priests and put under a Mayan temple to the Sun Godin Yucatan, Mexico.

BLUE alters are clone armies and the alters will self injure or kill itself to protect it from leaking information or being deprogrammed. Suicide programs to kill you by possibly having a heart attack or using a weapon on your self or physically exhausting the biology.

LIGHT BLUE alters are in charge of the way the system runs. Light blue protects the biology they are on the light side of the mostly dark alters.

DARK BLUE altersprotect the cult and are on the dark side.

WHITE are Atlantean alters who have been given Aryan racial stuff to think they are superior. WHITE are internal programmers that come around in white robes and white light. They believe in genetic engineering, and a master race, your basic Nazi plans during WW II that has NOT gone away and is the guideline for the New World Order and New World Religion, are you ready?

ORANGE are special protectors or scout alters that warn of internal or external threats. Guard alters are heavily programmed for obedience to the cult. They give out the warning when something bad is about to happen. When a slave is committing a criminal act in society they may internally or psychically be tipped off that the police are coming or they are in danger in some other way.

When the children are forced into prostitution rings at age four years and up the guard will let them know when a "John" plans to hurt them and they should run. The prostitution and drug running is to earn money for cult operations and the illuminati drugging and raping.

The abuser can also be a trainer or programmer and the guard will give the slave a "heads up." Some alters work for the biology, to keep it alive and some alters work for the cult, do as we tell you or die. No confusion in those orders.

YELLOW has a few strong Christian, front alters in the system to serve as a balancing point to the control System and HIDE what the System is all about. Yellow alters are ritually and sexually twinned with alters of other systems with OPPOSING spiritual belief in the Lord Jesus Christ of Nazareth.

The alters that believe in Jesus and that he will SAVE them get tormented by the alters in the blacks, purples, reds, and all the other alters who are mad that God didn't do anything to help them or rescue them.

The illuminati devised their programming to PREVENT their slave's from KNOWING what universal law says. You need to save your self. They keep their slaves and our religions arguing about being rescued or NOT. That way we never commune with our invisible aspects and align with universal law. We continue in our dark patterns not working on rescuing our self.

Universal Law of **PERPETUAL TRANSMUTATION of ENERGY** is that all humans have the power to change the conditions in their lives. Raising your vibration IS HARD work. You need to stay in your biology. Focus your thoughts and we ALL have the skill set to do that. What you have attracted you have to UNDO yourself.

PINK think they are core personality related alters that maintain the true feelings of the human apart from the cult. Pink are reporting alters and the tattletales. They call and report them self, even. They are the little innocent ones. They are emotionally very fragile.

These alters THINK they are the core personality but it is another illuminati lie to control their slaves. The real core personality is in hiding until the little human is brave enough to break and leave their programming behind them. The core personality is waiting for little human to get tired of being an illuminati puppet.

METAL and JEWEL Programming

METAL Programming is what many Illuminati children are given. Metals can be from bronze (lowest) to platinum (highest) and is laid in the same way jewel programming is.

JEWEL Programmingis similar to metal programming but higher level and more difficult to obtain. What level is put in and when, is dependent on the child's parents' status or DNA, the region it is born in, the group it is born into, and the trainers that work with it.

JEWEL programming is started at **2 or 3 years** of age and is considered higher than metals to achieve it and higher levels means more abuse, drugging, hypnotism and electro shock and control.

. The child is shown a piece of jewelry or a large example of the jewel (or metal) and asked isn't this amethyst, ruby, emerald or diamond beautiful? The child will be eager to look at it and touch it. To become a jewel you need to EARN the right with TRAINING and systematic abuse and trauma to create full alters inside.

Amethyst is usually 1st earned and linked to KEEPING SECRETS.

Ruby is next and linked to SEXUAL ABUSE and sexual alters inside. As the child is repeatedly sexually traumatized and survives they CREATE **sexual** alters to please adult perversions.

Emerald generally comes at ages 12 to 15 years and linked to family loyalty, WITCHCRAFT and dark spiritual achievement. Emeralds often have a black cat linked to them.

Diamond is the highest gemstone, and not all children will earn it. "Family jewels" are often passed down internally during training sessions with trainers and family members. All high Illuminati families will have jewels hidden in secret vaults, which have been passed down for generations.

Triads of three **elders** may be seen in the alter system. Platinum's may have a head council of three. Jewels will have a triad of ruby, emerald, diamond in many systems, torule over the others as an internal LEADERSHIP COUNCIL, "System Above", "AscendedMasters", "supreme council", regional council, world council, etc. may be found.

Jewels will have a triad, made up of ruby, emerald, diamond in many systems, to rule over the others as an internal "leadership council", "System Above", "Ascended Masters", "supreme council", regional council, world council, etc. may be found. The councils found will vary with each survivor. It is not uncommon for the survivor to incorporate a parent, both parents, and grandparents, into their internal leadership hierarchy in a generational survivor. High priests and priestesses may sit on ruling councils inside the internal system of alters.

Ask your invisible aspects if you have metal programming? Ask how that programming affects you today?

Chapter 3
FETAL TRAUMA

Why wait to make the childhood a living hell for the child, start before birth with your basic **FETAL TRAUMA** and Programming to encourage dissociation and demon possession before the baby is even born. Get the brain moving in the direction you want it to move BEFORE birth. The parents torture the fetus in the womb with thinneedles that are inserted through the mother's belly and uterus into the fetus. Specialized drugs and certain food and drink are used to cause trauma and upset to the mother and fetus, let DRAMA and TRAUMA become a lifestyle.

Mother and fetus can be SEVERELY traumatized during pregnancy by the spouse or cult members. For example the father may purposely abandon the pregnant mother in the middle of a forest or desert, what ever she fears most or blast the mother with loud frightening music and then follow this up with loving actions or physical abuse and then more loving actions. The mother's trauma is passed on to the fetus when her fear makes the uterus contract squeezing the fetus and the stress chemicals fed through umbilical cord will change with her emotional changes.

A premature birth is important to the illuminati because the naturally occurring events around a premature birth INSURE that the child is traumatized. The mother must push the baby through the birth canal alone because the premature birthing of the baby means it cannot help the mother in the small ways that a full term baby can. The strain on the heart of the mother is EXTREME.

Ask your invisible aspects if you have had fetal trauma, yes or no? Was it planned or accidental, yes or no? How does that trauma affect you now? Ask for a slide show, please.

The Illuminati has learned that a mother can usually give 2 or 3 preemie births like this before she risks death. Generational satanic families are given to Satan. The fetus and child are given family demons along with the family CURSES. The Moonchild rituals are the rituals to demonize a fetus. The demons that are invoked to enter the child are large and very powerful and include layering in of their demonic forces with blood ritual. All are low vibrating dark demons to give "the little human" the illusion of greater and darker power.

KNOW the power is only in the lower vibration of unconsciousness and darkness. The "fear energy" that all darkness feeds from is always present in their slaves and on earth. That explains the tension in the biology of illuminati slaves and the big eyes they have. The eyes that look like they cannot believe what horrible things they have seen and felt.

Ask your invisible aspects if you had demons put in you as an infant yes or no? A DEMONis an entity that is 70-100% dark.

If you are not part of the illuminati and your family abused you because they were abused and it is acceptable behavior in your family to abuse the child, one of your DARK dead relatives could easily possess your biology and be considered a demon. Dark entities like to help you put yourself down, get you in trouble and make you feel stupid so you carry less light and they can enter your biology when they like and control it. They like to do what they did when they had biology.

When you dissociate you invite in dark entities by default. That becomes your choice consciously or unconsciously.

Ask your invisible aspects what percentage of the time you are possessed.

Are you blaming a demon for your inappropriate behavior BECAUSE you allowed it to enter you and take over your consciousness? That was a free will CHOICE on your part. When you own a thing you can change it.

LIFESTYLE

Abandonment, indifference, being traumatized and comforted and used by your caretakers as an infant and toddler can seriously mess the individual up in all their personal relationships throughout life. You can imagine what a charming parent they will make. This pattern of push away, abuse, ignores and great loving feelings from the important people in your life makes NO SENSE to a child or adult. It is all endless DRAMA and TRAUMA you never feel SAFE or loveable. Your whole world is nutty and scary. The emotional age of an infant, child or adult is arrested at age 2 to 3 years. To grow emotionally you would need stability and safety.

The new soul groups that came in with higher vibrations and more spiritual awareness, to help crumble the dark illuminati are not as easily programmed but some really do not handle our dark ways very well and are crumbling them self and becoming part of the problem.

This "nutty set" of behaviors the illuminati has or they would say well thought out and it works to control others and create human robots. The illuminati methods make it al-

most impossible to have an intimate "healthy" close relationship with anyone ESPECIALLY your self. The illuminati want
an obedient skilled slave that won't bond with their invisible
aspects. A good worker is totally shut off from their feelings. The only TIGHT relationships I see in the illuminati are
very dysfunctional and controlling relationships with a father
and daughter or father and son or mother and son NEVER
mother and daughter, they just hate each other as they are
supposed to do. Female bonding is never liked or encour-
aged. NO "we are women, hear us roar" in the illuminati.

There is a program used to make two females appear
they are bonding for one to get secrets from the other. For
example a mother may start confiding secret things to a
daughter, real or imagined. The things she confides may be
lies or not. The purpose is to get the daughter to betray any
secrets they may have been keeping.

Some of the other tools of the illuminati trainer uses
to handle small ones and all ages is the "trainer table" that is
frequently a steel table covered with plastic or easily cleaned
material. On the sides at intervals are restraints for arms,
legs and neck to prevent movement. Trainer's chair is a large
chair with arm rests and it will have restraints for arms, legs
and neck to prevent movement while a person sits in the
chair. Other trainer tools include steel instruments to insert
into orifices to cause pain, STRETCH machines used as punishment stretches a person without breaking bones and is
extremely painful.

Comfort objects for victims like stuffed animals or oils
for massage. Warm towels and beverages as the trainer
bonds with the person they worked with. Trainer grids and

projectors to project grids on wall or ceiling, Journals with indexed copies of the slaves systems and command codes.

The parents are the trainers and administer **TODDLER Programming** in illuminati families. The parent is often the "trainer" and "handler" at home. At 15 to 18 months of age there is more fragmenting and dissociating the child sees over and over again the same parent endanger their life and then will rescue them. The parent intermittently sooth and bond with the toddler and then shock the fingers, toes and genitals.

The infant may be dropped from heights to a mat and is TERRIFIED and crying. Then the adults laugh at the infant's pain and distress. The child may be placed in cages for periods of time at home and during rituals and training.

A parent will hold the child's head under water until they all but drown and then the parent rescues them. Ah, the hero again. Then there is the daily anal raping which makes the infant go unconscious. As the child gets older and doesn't pass out you slap them so all they remember is the physical abuse. The slap is a focus changer, a trigger to bring in a different alter that only remembers the slap and never the VIOLENT sexual assault of the infant.

The illuminati parent rapes their newborn male and female children anally because all our 13 meridians that connect humans to their invisible aspects meet in the rectum. The illuminati want to destroy that connection. The illuminati cannot access the 13 meridian connections themselves because they vibrate too low to do that. The forces of creation had to hide that power so humans wouldn't hurt themselves like they did in Sodom and Gomorrah.

Your invisible aspects will know what REALLY happened.

Ask your invisible aspects if your physical abuse in child-hood was used to HIDE larger traumas, yes or no? Are you open and aware enough to ask for a slide show or feeling show of what was hidden from your awareness?

Have you been traumatized and comforted by the same person many times yes or no? Has experiencing these two extremes from the same person over and over again enabled you to have very unstable relationships as an adult and YOU are very unstable as an adult? Has this destroyed your ability to have any relationship? Is it possible for you to trust anyone or you, yes or no?

Do you attach yourself to another person for a week or two and do everything they do with them and one day you have NO contact with them for weeks or months and you have no idea why, I wonder where you would have learned such inconsistent, unreliable behavior.

The **DEHUMANIZATION Programming** like ever bit of this "training" isn't dehumanizing. This programming creates alters that are animals or things. Young children are led to believe they ARE various types of animals like a bird, cat, dog, alien, horse, earth element, gemstone, rock, and countless other items to insure that the alter continues to believe they are not human.

All the Disney productions from the early 1900s until present time have been designed and used for this type of programming and triggering of children and adults. The chil-dren shows on television reinforce a child being the wind or water or dragon, on and on.

For example the trainer may want to create a cat alter. Bring on the drugs, electro-shock and hypnosis. The child "in its cage" drugged and electro-shocked over and over is asked, if it wants to become a cat? They are told cats never get killed and tortured like CHILDREN do. In the same space the trainer and child are, there is cages of little girls that are dirty and tortured and ill fed. When the child "agrees" to be a cat they are forced to eat like cats with cats and are repeatedly SHAMED, degraded and told they are cats.

I have had public school students that sat under tables and meowed and refused to come out or talk. I guess the "trainer" messed up the FRONT alters.

A lie detector is hooked up to the child to determine if the alter believes it is a cat. A great deal of simple torture is applied to make sure that the correct answers are given to the trainer and believed. No one is trusted and nothing is left to chance.

High-speed films of kittens playing and having fun are shown in one eye, while the other eye is forced to see little girls having to undergo the worst of tortures. This viewing is forced upon the child as its eyes are held open and the child is strapped into a viewing chair. More hypnosis and drug induced states are used.

The painful rape of a child with its legs held in a butterfly configuration is used to get a butterfly alter. To get a puppet, the body is given a drug to paralyze the child. Then electroshock is applied to certain muscles upon the command of the programmer. The effect is that the child has no control over his body, and the programmer can make the child's body parts jerk and move by electro-shocking them.

Every aspect of being in the illuminati is dehumanizing.

You NEVER are given a chance to be your own person.

That is why you need to be dissociated to stay a member of the satanic cult or "illuminated ones" just as most of our politicians are and those managing OUR money are, the media and performers are mostly dissociated. There is just no one home. The public wants to be just like them, how very sad. Have you noticed the pathology in their personal life and the same issues that are created over and over for the illuminati "trained"?

DISNEY the man, movies and entertainment parks has been a major contributor to the deceptions and abuses of the Illuminati a member in good standing. Disney have some well maintained angelic front alters. Disney was raised in illuminati style and was an active Satanist. He harassed landowners and stolen employee idea's. Disney ranked 48 by Forbes in the top 500 companies. He created HARD PORN, snuff films, and witchcraft.

Disney cartoons, movies and stories have always been used by programmers especially the wizard of Oz. Disney was asked to design stories around what the programmers wanted to reinforce in the child and to trigger the child. Role-playing the different characters in Disney films reinforced programming.

Military programming may be linked to Star Wars. Computer programming may be linked to Hal in 2001 A Space Odyssey; internal labyrinth programming may link to the movie Labyrinth. The program will be ground in with repetition, electroshock, TOURTURE, drugging and hypnosis. The alters inside who have gone through this programming will often be highly disconnected from external reality and may believe that they are part of a SCRIPT like Dorothy seeking the Emerald City or the achievement of Illuminati rule on earth. They may be a computer or the character Data in Star Wars.

WAKE UP and start feeling and sensing what is going on.

That is why we need to go back to childhood traumas to FEEL what was true so we can integrate and heal it as a part of our experience. That is why your invisible aspects are bringing these memories back to you now to KNOW what really happened and own it. To move to higher vibrations and OUT of the illuminati vibration you must integrate your self now or wait for the next 26,000-year cycle to roll around again and try it then.

The **DENIAL Programming** goes like this, today the child was horrendously wounded and TRAUMATIZED and the next morning everyone connected to the abuse acts as if nothing happened. How can a toddler EVER know what is real. In my experience the toddler becoming an adult still does not know what is real. The family models a lifestyle of DENIAL and irrational behavior for the infant and young child. The average dysfunctional family operates in denial all the time just like the addicted do, like the sexually addicted and the substance abuser does.

You do not need to even ask you invisible aspects if you have had some denial programming, but you could ask what percentage of the time you function in denial today.

DENIAL is NEVER a strength or asset. Denial is a choice to HIDE other choices and avoid owning your feelings. Judgment is a form of denial. When you narrow your focus small enough to judge only an aspect of someone or something you avoid knowing about what you do not want to know or feel about your SELF. You avoid focus on your inability to be compassionate and loving to YOU. The greater your need to deny or dissociate the more distorted and twisted things get in your life.

DECEPTIONis a POWERLESS response. Being honest and truthful increases your self-worth. SELF-LOVE creates patience, compassion and understanding towards the self and others.

Own your deceptions and what you deny so you can have control over it or nothing will change. Denial, self-deception and dissociation are in reality CONDONING the behavior. The higher vibration on earth since December 2009 has interfered with our ability to deny and when we try to deny, it is still in our face or consciousness or awareness and its NOT going away.

DRUG MOVEMENT

Infants and children are drugged all the time in the illuminati and how does that affect their small-undeveloped biologies and brains and who cares about that? How surprising is it that they use drugs as adults. Then consider the effects of endless electric shock on a little biology. It is not uncommon for trainers to give too much electricity and destroy programming and the child's ability to be a good slave and sometimes live. How many have died from too many drugs? Most all of the children died that they used to test radiation. The few that lived have many challenges to deal with daily. I think you get the picture of how all this affects the growing child's ability to function and live in present time. When the child or adult gets out of control by not being a good slave they stop living one way or another, an accidental death or a body to eat ritualistically.

The CIA and Illuminati programming centers have more than 600 to 700 different drugs at their disposal. They can make a person feel like he or she is in heaven, or burning in hell or make the person vomit. If they want a little girl to have breasts they give her hormones. To create a raving paranoia in a person you give them too much dopamine or too little dopamine. Reduce serotonin and they will be unable to understand cause and effect.

Thorazine was used regularly at the CIA's Jonestown, Guyana GROUP control experiment in mind control. Many drugs especially experimental ones are only known by code names. The drugs can be used with elaborate light, sound and motion shows that produce whatever effect the programmer wants to produce like the sensation of SHRINK-ING or dying.

Drugs or Electroconvulsive shock are used to destroy memory in slaves after they have done a mission for the Illuminati. Drugs and ECS are used, as the slap is used to change your focus. The focus change method is largely the personal taste of the programmer, controller or handler.

Retroactive amnesia is the inability to retrieve or recall information before the traumatic event and that can be created with a shot of Acetoxycycloheximide, cyclohexamide, or puromyxcin under the skin. A more sophisticated technique incorporates the drug seconal, dissociation and hypnosis. Remember that children can start their JOBS for the illuminati at and around two years of age.

Your invisible aspects remember what happened to you. Ask them for a slide show of what happened before you were given the drug focus changer.

Where does all the money come from?

Funding for COVERT PROJECTS of the CIA and illuminati are from illegal drug trade around the world. Who do you suppose runs all those operations. Why are they unable to stop them? They do not want to stop the drug trade and other criminal activity. The more the laws are tightened by the so-called "War on Drugs," the higher the street value is for the drugs. The American authorities have allowed US Oil companies to ship chemicals to South America and other agencies. They transport drugs from South America by sea to oilrigs drilling off the US coast. From there they could be brought ashore under the cover of the oil operations. It came very close to becoming widely known in the wake of the Iran-Contra Affair and now with the gulf oil spill. Those who have investigated the CIA-drug connection say it began in the late 1950s and has not stopped.

Another large money source is the high quality videos and DVD's devoted to kiddy-porn, "pedophile entertainment," degrading treatment, coprophilia for those that get sexually aroused by excretions, torture, rape and death, which Satanists have always produced. Many Toilet Sex starlets are committed Satanists and Alpha Lodge members or affiliates.

GOVERNMENT Programming installed in illuminati slaves is used to infiltrate local political parties and those running for leadership positionslocally and nationally or working for top leaders as ADMINISTRATORS, financialadvisors funding governmental races and backing the person sympathetic tothe Illuminati or putting their person in to win. Eventually causing thedownfall of all major governments in the world and then installing the New World Order and

New World Religion. They already control our financial markets, the media and most religions.

CIA Programming uses brain wave and color-coding. These programs were developed through military research and funding in 1950—1960's. Alters were trained to become hyper aware of conversations even when whispered. INTERNAL human recorders are taught to download these conversations. Photographic recall is emphasized and downloaded.

MILITARY Programming is being emphasized and installed by the Illuminati as part of their plan to takeover the world. Currently all cult children are undergoing some form of military training at 3 years with simple exercises. Parents take the children to a training area that may be a "large inside auditorium" or remote outside area to do training maneuvers. They march in time and keep straight lines and what fun would any of this be without being PUNISHED by being kicked, electric shocked with cattle prods or beaten with a baton.

They are dressed in small uniforms like the adults. The adults have ranks, badges and insignia indicating their level of achievement in the illuminati cult hierarchy and military. They spend hours learning to aim, sight, and fire guns to condition them to KILLING. They are shown violent films of warfare more explicit and graphic than normal movies, video games and virtual reality play. Killing techniques are shown in slow motion "kill or be killed" gets ground in over and over.

War games for older youths are used and the losers are punished. We are so surprised. They are taught to leave behind the weak or slow members. Unfit members are killed. The goal is to create, creative cognitive leaders inside the military systems who DISSOCIATE under stress, which triggers programs. An honorable soldier will take his life rather than reveal secrets or leave his unit.

Ask your invisible aspects if you have had sleeper military training, yes or no? Ask what trigger will activate your program? Ask your invisible aspects to give you CONSCIOUS awareness of you being triggered so you will KNOW what has happened inside your self and stay aware in present time so YOU are in control instead of allowing your programming to be in control.

VIRTUAL REALITY Programming uses a virtual reality headset, suit and illuminati produced VR disc. The disc uses holographic images, scripted programs and targets with practice sequences for assassintraining. Under hypnosis and drugs the person thinks it is real. Virtually any scenario can be recreated and reinforced over and over. The VR disc is more advanced than any video or arcade games.

The CONTROLLERS

I know people that talk about mind control and being programmed give warnings to the reader or viewer about having their programming triggered or restimulated. My thought on the subject is good let us trigger your programming so you can have conscious awareness of what you do and take control of it. Awareness heals you. All you need do is STOP dissociating and you can control your programming and be in charge of what you do by staying in present time ALL THE TIME. Alignment WITH the universal laws and working with your invisible aspects will raise your vibration up and OUT of the LOW illuminati vibration.

The ILLUMINATI are the generational satanic blood-lines and they are the power behind the secret societies and most governments and religions on earth. They direct their operations from behind the scenes. Within the illuminati on all levels there are warring factions. The center of power resides in the lower 4th dimension in the "clear ones" that give everyone else orders. Every president elected from George Washington in 1789 on, has been won by the illuminati.

The top of the illuminati pyramid consist of the 13 ruling families and each is given an area or function to fulfill. For example GLOBAL FINANCE, mind control, military or technology research and development, media, entertainment and news or religion. Number 13 is considered the highest level of knowledge. Each ruling family has a council of 13. All 13 families are shape shifters or hybrids 50% human and 50% or more reptilian. The layer below the 13 ruling families in the hierarchy, support the ruling families and are called the committee of 300.

The committee of 300 is not all hybrid reptilians but do have a higher percent of reptilian DNA than most humans have, which is around 15 to 20%. The committee of 300 uses many well known PRIVATE institutions to further the reptilian agenda including the Council of Foreign relations, Mafia, CIA, NSA, Secret Service, Federal Reserve, International Affairs, Internal Revenue Service and Interpol are just a few of their front organizations.

The BASIC ILLUMINATI PROGRAMMING is based upon Illuminati and Nazi goals to create a Master race in part through GENETICS and mostly through control and force. Mind-controlled slaves are given multifunctional programming and usually are used to help program other slaves.

Parents program children. These children will often receive lavish experiences as well as talks to convince them that they are part of the ELITE. Maybe they aren't part of the elite mostly slaves are lied to and manipulated endless.

By 4 years of age the child has been tested many times in many ways. Including the PERSONALITY ASSESSMENT SYSTEM or PAS designed by John Gittinger and is to evaluate BABY'S current and future personality. There are 3 major axes that can be graphed to describe a baby's personality. Based on the PAS a programmer would automatically know the child will become a SOCIAL or RELIGIOUS reformer. The child's programming charts would then be labeled some suitable occupation such as "Environmental Activist", "Pentecostal church reformer", "Consumer Advocate", or "Activist against Narcotics."

The programming for that child then would follow, 6-month goals to develop that mind-controlled slave into one of the best in that occupation. The child's weaknesses and strengths are charted and the child's destiny in life is determined. The chart has the occupation the child will be CREATED for and what their function will be in the overall Illuminati plan. Their programs are determined and the appropriate alters will be created. The map of the Land of Oz in the Wizard of Oz books was frequently used for the front alters. A system built as a city of entities having unity and multiplicity.

Ask your invisible aspects what you were programmed to do for the illuminati?

The universal law of **DIVINE MANIFESTATION** is win-win-win-win to benefit all involved and harm done to none. Any harm to another in the process or outcome of manifestation is not DIVINE and carries karmic debt.

To execute the plans of the illuminati, it takes many, many handlers, trainers and controllers. The older dissociated ones need to control and instruct the younger dissociated ones and there is your unity. Slaves controlling each other, a dissociated society operating with controlled minds and thoughts passed on to the young. You just need to call forth the right alter.

The mothers do the earliest sexual training for all the children even all the sexual positions are taught and drawn. Teachers in schools wonder where very young students learned to draw explicit sexual acts. They learned it at home of course. There is no free will or thinking for your self. Never forget endless drugging, electric shock and violence if you do not play the game right, how to twist the meaning of unity into forced unity and perversion and twisted darkness.

The universal law of CAUSE and EFFECT or RECIPRO-CAL action is that nothing happens by CHANCE or outside of universal laws. Every action has a reaction or consequence. You get back what you give ALL the TIME so be conscious of your emanations. IT IS NOT personal it is physics. Keep functioning at a survival level with the illuminati and you will keep attracting survival situations to master for your spiritual awareness on that level.

A HANDLER is an "energy construct" that CONTROLS the fabric of a being or entity that has the ABILITY to be CONSCIOUS. The concept of being a handler, teacher, instructor, coach or trainer is a neutral concept. The intent of a particular handler can certainly be dark or light, compassionate or violent and anything in between.

The illuminati put in alters that act as internal handlers and they can be dark or light to keep the system balanced some. ALONG with the internal handlers there are many human handlers and trainers to control their slaves. For example one lady had two dark internal handlers that happened to be the cults idea of her mother and grandmother that taught and enforced "family loyalty" FIRST, not the blood family but the cult family. In the same woman there is a light internal handler hiding out waiting to help her but hasn't come out yet. She has several human handlers and sometimes more.

FREQUENTLY handlers handle the unconscious or dissociated human or a demon possession could be considered a handler. Handlers can be another human controlling or enabling the unconscious and dissociated individual or an addiction can be handling a human. Belief's' adopted from religions teachings or other doctrines the individual has been exposed to may be controlling them and act as a handler. Someone vibrating low WILL distort and twist whatever they learn to serve their own personal need like some religious fanatics do. Even a dead family member or demon is an entity that has 30% to no light and can possesses your biology at times. Dark entities or handlers like to help you put yourself down to lower your vibration and keep you depressed so it is easier to enter your biology and control it when they like.

The universal law of PERPETUAL TRANSMUTATION of ENERGY is that all humans have the power to change the conditions in their lives. Raising your vibration is hard work. You need to stay in your biology to do that. Focus your thoughts and we ALL have the skill set to do that. What you have attracted you have to UNDO yourself.

The MONARCH Programming was a specific project carried out by secret elements of the U.S. government and intelligence groups. There are 40,000 actively monitored Monarch slaves.

The Illuminati and other organizations have also programmed individuals who are simply EXPENDABLE sex slaves used up and killed very early in life. One-time use saboteurs, breeders, soldiers, drug couriers and so forth. The expendable ones are the children of parents who were blackmailed into turning their children over to the CIA and hadn't been programmed since birth. The CIA and Illuminati watched for porn in the mail and now on the internet and those who are found abusing their SMALL children and give them a choice of going to prison or cooperate with them by selling their children to them.

The National Security Act hides the information about who was blackmailed and who was purchased. The CIA is a front for the Illuminati and they set up fronts like that in many state mental hospitals and McGill Psychiatric Training Network that consists of eight Montreal hospitals, especially St. Mary's, NASA in Huntsville, Alabama, the Presidio in California; and NOTS at China Lake in California, to name a few. Satanists within the Network and the CIA took over Boy's Town in Nebraska in the early 1950s, to be sure of a constant supply of boys for programming and sexual use. This information is taken from Bloodlines of Illuminati by:Fritz Springmeier, 1995

The PRINCIPLE of JOY and INNER PEACE increases with each deeper connection of the little human and their invisible aspects. This process of surrender and allowing and giving up human free will for living in divine will with your invisible aspects with all your alters integrated.

Chapter 4
MESSAGES from?

Creating alters and splits is carefully orchestrated with drugs, hypnosis, lights, pictures, words and sounds. Electric shock and implants, humiliation and violent abuse help also. The neuron network of the brain of slaves is purposely distorted to keep the alters from reconnecting and staging a revolution or integration. When you stay away from handlers and suicide programs a slave that fells safe at times can start integrating their alters and walk away from their controllers and all the nuttiness and control of their mind and biology.

TRACKING IMPLANTShave been given to animals, military personnel, civilians and objects including cardiovascular filters, defibrillators, pacemaker electrodes, heart valves, tracheal prostheses, breathing monitors, portable oxygen generators, ventilators, infusion oxygen generators, ventilators, infusion pumps and various silicone gel-filled devices as testicular and breast implants and spinal implants. Tracking implants have a life span of 250 years. They will probably last longer than you will.

AUDIO implants began to be publicly placed into people in the 1960s. The military in and during the Vietnam War used auditory implant devices to aid communicating with their men. Many of these implant victims had programmed multiple personalities or Dissociative Identity disorder since birth. They were raised in the illuminati. The controllers were very heavy handed with the people they implanted and they used the full force of the Illuminati Intelligence agencies power to keep these people under their control at all times.

The innocent victims have had their lives totally destroyed some tried to fight back from underneath the incessant audio messages that the implants sent. The illuminati saw to it that no one would help these individuals. Not the police, doctors, congressmen, psychologists and many others were NOT ALLOWED to help victims and some had their suicide programs activated. During the 1970s through the 80s, medical researchers kept putting more and more audio implants into deaf and hard of hearing individuals. Hundreds in the United States and other countries received the cochlear implants.

MESSAGES

Messages from implants, angels, guides, aliens, or ascended masters can be from your controller or handler or the government with a device or psychically. With all the drugs, abuse, hypnosis and low frequency vibrations with messages hitting us how can we know what is real and from what source? How do you know what is true, when you are getting a sound and light show mostly you are being entertained. As your attention is diverted outward and you allow your attention to be held there you get diverted from your invisible aspects and what they have to share with you and what knowingness is being sent to your senses.

Your discernment is continually being tested. If you abandoned your biology or are living in the past or future you aren't getting the sensory information your invisible aspects are sending your way.

Not knowing about your programming or the fact that you were raised in an illuminati family is an illusion also.

Inside you know.

Ask your invisible aspects if you are aware of your programming yes or no? Then ask what percent of the time you are aware of it?

With alters changing all the time it is a challenge to take conscious control of the many different aspects you may have. Staying in your biology and in present time is the only way to go if you care to crash your programming. If you weren't raised in the illuminati but your family was dark and dysfunctional the only way to break their hold on you is to stay in your biology and present time and make your OWN choices. Walk away from the abusers they do NOT play fair and NEVER will; you will get sucked in over and over again. Fight with dark and you will lose. You win ONLY when you walk away and let them be on the path they choose.

You need to commit to you and your invisible aspects.

Several more programs to distort and twist a slave's reality and make them dissociate are "upside-down" and "silence" programs.

UPSIDE DOWN Programming is hanging or being suspended upside down for one or two hours. That will play TRICKS on the MIND and it starts to dissociate and reverse PAIN and PLEASURE. This is often done with Beta alters to get them to think that painful sadistic rape, an illuminati favorite, is pleasurable. After reversals you get PAIN IS LOVE and the sadomasochistic kitten alters beg for more abuse to excuse the predators guilt and to prevent the predator from remembering when they were programmed and how much they suffered.

Remember that the vibration of terror, pain and suffering FEEDS energy to the reptilians in the illuminati. That energy siphoning creates the illusion that they are powerful because they can terrorize the helpless.

Ask your invisible aspects for a slide show of dark feeding from your terror and trauma.

SILENCE Programming is trauma to force SILENCE by repeatedly killing humans of all ages in front of the infant or child being programmed whiletelling the mind-control victim the people are being sadistically killed because they talked. Nice way to keep people terrorized and confused.

Ask your invisible aspects for a slide show of the killings you have seen. The killings you have been forced to take part in.

New agers say we can send the dark away or WALL them off and that is not true. We function in a free will zone and are responsible for ALL OUR experiences and aspects. To make consistently LIGHT choices and align with universal law you will need to be very alert at first until you get the hang of who is saying what in your head and who is your aspect and how light, they are.

UNCONSCIOUS thought

Yes 74% of the earth's population is unconscious, negative, dark and only able to carry zero to 30% of their light, which represents the percentage of communication they may have with their invisible aspects and the amount of alignment they may have with universal laws.

How to deal with living in that much darkness?

Do NOT upset yourself about it.

Do not organize against the dark or try to fight the unconscious ones.

Do not try to change the unconscious or anyone because it will result in your going darker. The "unconscious, 74%" of the population have free will and have made that choice until they make other choices so stay away from them. The unconscious may ask for help. If you think you have something to offer they will grasp, by all means help. Otherwise walk away. They have free will.

You want to raise your vibration to lift yourself out of their vibration. Focus on that and alignment with universal law.

The universal law of **ALLOWING** means dropping ALL judgment, blame and emotional attachment to what others DO, SAY or think. They are on their own spiritual path with their invisible aspects. Allowing requires granting others, even children the right to BE just as they are, doing whatever THEY choose. Children do need to be protected and supported. With higher vibrational thought, truths and self-love we evolve out of the circle of darkness, force and control. TOLERANCE is not allowing it is holding negative thoughts.

PRINCIPLE of **PROJECTION** is that the story of one's life and concurrent lives are stored within you and can only be changed or rewritten from within you by changing your thoughts. The intimate conversations, beliefs and relationship one has are reflected in experiences on the outer screen of their life. We are both the camera and projector of our own life story. Those wishing to see joyous experiences instead of reruns, trash films, soap operas, tragedies, illness and hostilities, must refuse to bring or allow such films, concepts or images to fill their storage banks and unconsciousness with them.

The universal law of **ATTRACTION** says the thoughts and emotions of the little human create a vibrational energy consciously or unconsciously that emanates from us and attracts like energy. The universe does not care if your emanations are real or IMAGINED, negative or positive. It simply reflects with CLARITY and TRUTH what is held in your energy field. Moving to the larger realities and truths enable us to release our rage, anger and frustration. The human is a temporary vehicle and was never designed to RULE we are here to experience.

DEMON messages

Demon messages come from a variety of sources, family, friends, school, religious institutions songs, television and programming formal and informal. Demons are ANY source that carries only 30% light to no light. That would be 50% of the population on this planet currently.

The PHI THETA OMEGA Programmingis adding dark SPIRITUAL alters, demon possession, internal witches, warlocks, seers, psychics, readers, occult practitioners, family members and handlers are all in this system of highly developed right brain and deep trance abilities.

The color is coded BLACK. The training is most commonly done from ages 8 to 21 years with occasional reinforcement of the programming from time to time. Brain wave training is complex and creates automatic amnesia and communication barriers between the different brain wave states. This is reinforced by electric SHOCK and punishment to prevent its undoing. All brain wave systems have CON-

TROLLER triads considered more "mystical" stable and un-breakable, three back ups and three system controllers.

PORCELAIN FACE or BURNING Programming is part of the Camelot and Shakespeare program to steal an alters face. Fire torture and melted wax is used to make the child victim believe their face has been burned off. The programmer gives the traumatized alter a porcelain mask to wear. The Illuminati victim wears this mask when they are married to the Anti-Christ or Satan or EL.

The satanic network "**Assembly of God** churches" also uses the burning or porcelain face programming. They put a wax mask upon the victim, and give them fire torture. They think their face has melted. The programmer pretends to be a "god" and gives them a new face or porcelain mask and the memories of abuse are then hypnotically hidden behind the mask. To take off the mask is to burn again or re-member the pain again.

Ask your invisible aspects if one of your aspects has married Satan yes or no? Can you have a sideshow?

Ask your invisible aspects if you have a porcelain face? Does it prevent your awareness of pain and abuse?

GAMMA Programmingis the secret layering in of demons. The ceremonies to demonize the victim occur even before they are born. Generational dark entities or demons are layered in to work with the direction of the programming. This 10th science deals with occult sciences of astral projection, ESP and telepathy. Gamma code calls for demons and SUICIDE programming is often layered into this system. These alternate personalities would rather DIE than leave their FAMILY or cult.

In gamma there is also Scholarship programming and photographic memory. Gamma alters know 8 different languages some modern and ancient.

Ask your invisible aspects how many languages you know?

GATEKEEPERS are found throughout the illuminati system. They are to impose their reality on other alters within the system with SUPPRESSION, judgments, control and deception. They do not ALLOW freedom of thought just like the illuminati won't allow free thought.

Ask your invisible aspects the number of gatekeepers you have? Are any of them human? Gatekeepers are NOT aligned with the universal law of free will.

The universal law of **FREE WILL** is divine will granting each entity the right to DIRECT and PURSUE his or her life so long as he or she does not violate the same right of others. A right that excludes the rights of others is NOT DIVINE.

EARTH BOUND or SHADOW PEOPLE or DEMONS

The earth bound are an essence without biology. They can appear shadow like or you sense or see their presence. Generally we haven't seen them because their vibration is SLIGHTLY out of our range of sight at this time. The "autistic" generally can see them and sense their presence because their range of sight is greater. If the earthbound happens to be a person that controlled you in life, like your mother and they have not gone to the bridge of flowers yet, they may still be trying to control or possess you.

For example, the dead grandfather was the leader of his cult and he would possess the granddaughter 80% of the time because he wanted to continue controlling his group and partake in all the sexual perversions he enjoyed as a cult leader in life. The grandfather possessing the granddaughter so often made her life pretty miserable. Sometimes grandfather possessed the men that the granddaughter had sex with including her husband.

The granddaughter was eventually able to talk grandfather, his wife and some followers into crossing over to the bridge of flowers. That certainly gave her more control over herself, more peace and increased the amount of light she was able to carry.

Many earthbound just drop by to say Hi!

Some stay earthbound to learn more from the humans that are experiencing the higher vibrations and the movement into oneness.

Some earthbound do not realize they are dead or have unfinished business or are so attached to CONTROLLING their STUFF like a piece of land or a building or room they do not want to move on.

One man died leaving his wife and his money. He was very concerned about what she would do with his money. He hung around to watch her spend his money and he upset himself about that. Some controlling spirits in life continue the same way in death blaming and judging others and they refuse to cross over or go to the light until they have what they feel is justice. Death changes little in their essence and they probably weren't wronged but they failed to see the bigger picture and understand the way universal law works.

You can help the earthbound by giving them the date 2010 and a summary of what has happened to update them and increase their awareness of the time that has passed. Ask them if they would like you to help them go to the bridge of flowers and you can take them across. 80% of those that die get lost in the fourth dimension or the gray world. That is so uncomfortable for them they continue the cycle of taking biology, dying and going back to the fourth dimension.

UNIVERSAL ENERGY or COSMIC FLOW or INTELLIGENCE is the base energy that permeates all life in the universe or cosmos and is infinite. This is unconditional love energy with NO agenda or attachments. It has the highest vibration there is and flows a sense of wellbeing, compassion and knowingness through our invisible aspects or 90%er and then to the human. When you vibrate too low and carry only 20% light or less your invisible aspects cannot flow much energy to you and you may not be able to receive it. When you stop carrying light energy, To STAY ALIVE you will start feeding off the energy of anyone you can siphon energy or light from, just like the illuminati and clear ones do.

When they run out of light or fear energy to siphon the dark ones and earthbound move into the FALL PATH to oblivion. They can't get any universal energy and feed off each other eventually disintegrating into basic elements and become space dust. Their many small negative choices and vampirism ways fail to produce energy for them eventually.

ZERO-POINT energy is the measurement of universal energy at rest. When you are aware of it initially it feels like being stuck because there is no motion but this is the most powerful point a person can attain.

Universal energy BLENDSeverything together as the photon belt is doing at this time along with raising the planets vibration. Earth is in the process of twisting and contorting against the dark illuminati bonds that try to rule her and that is why we are feeling earthquakes and seeing volcano's erupt.

COMPLIANCE is the easiest way to steal another's energy. When you comply with darkness and serve their agenda they steal your energy. That includes family members and the illuminati. The energy stealing crosses to the NEXT lifetime and in-between each lifetime setting up a cycle of hopelessness in its victims. It bleeds into our SOUL energy and is a way to enslave or entrap the soul and create wicked karmic energies between two or more individuals.

From the child's point of perception that has no control and can be accessed at anytime by someone bigger or stronger that wants to touch, feel or force things into the child's orifices, like their mouth or bottom. The adult is so out of control they do not care about the child's welfare because no one ever rescued them when the adult was a child and forced.

The body of a child can be stimulated over and over again in many different ways to cause sexual arousal. A child that has not reached puberty can be sexually stimulated absolutely! Satanic cult members sexually traumatize, stimulate and drug all the children they can get a hold of especially their own children. This keeps the child sexually AROUSED but unable to do much about the arousal, as they are physically unable to orgasm until puberty. How much do you enjoy sexual arousal with no physical release? For the child to release their sexual tension or arousal they will need to physically exhaust themselves or distract themselves. Sexual tension or arousal is too distracting to focus your attention on much of anything BUT

SEX. The PARENT'S that sexually arouse their children wonder why the child can't learn at school and why the child starts fights. That is hard to figure out?

Being sexually stimulated and unable to focus mentally is a hard way to go through school and learn anything. The predator tells the child, "See you want it," and the child goes into GUILT, SHAME and BLAME. A great set up to torment the child the rest of its life, and a great rational and compulsion to seduce the next generation into sexual obsession and addiction.

When someone uses you sexually over a period of time and suddenly stops because you got too old, you will probably have some abandonment issues. It never dawns on a child that they just got "too old" to "sexually turn on" by a twisted fearful adult. So they spend the rest of their life trying to figure out what is wrong with THEM! If sexual activity is your only warm contact with other people you WILL MISS IT and feel abandoned when it is over and stops.

You may have come into this lifetime to help heal your mom's pathological physical, verbal and sexual abuse of her children. You as her child failed to change her even a little. Using the child's logic that the child has control of others, you spend your adult life hooking up with women OR men who abuse their children and you fail equally as bad as you did with mom or dad.

The change needs to come from WITHIN you and it needs to be FOR YOU not someone else. They need to make their own choices for them self. You carrying there darkness benefits no one. You deciding for another what they should do makes you darker. Them complying with your wishes makes you both darker.

The universal law of **CAUSE and EFFECT or RE-CIPROCAL action** is that nothing happens by CHANCE or outside of universal laws. Every action has a reaction or consequence. You get back what you give ALL the TIME so be conscious of your emanations. IT IS NOT personal it is physics. Keep functioning at a survival level and carrying others dark energy you will keep attracting survival situations to master for your spiritual awareness on that level.

There can be SPIRITUAL perks when you volunteer to go into an abusive family to improve things. Almost a 100% of children being born into sexually abusive situations volunteered for that to help a family work OUT of it. The sexual abuse goes on generation after generation in the same family. Only 25% actually succeed in changing things in the family some. Usual what happens is that the DARK family members win out while alive and afterwards. The person living gets overwhelmed and depressed by the earth bound entities darkness and they get darker.

The universal law of **ENTRAINMENT** REQUIRES that two resonances or vibrations existing in the same location MUST adjust and combine to have a single resonance. For Example, on a scale of 1-10 if one individual is at 3 and the other is at a 7 the law of entrainment requires that they will both be at 5 ish. The other possibility is when one resonance is overpowering it will pull the other to their level so you both would move to 3,4 or 6,7.

Every thought we have creates energetic ripples. Our body anchors our energetic layers, which fan out in every direction in ever-widening circles of vibrating frequency at six feet from the biology. The PRINCIPLE of Reconciliation and / or entrainment allows different qualities to get unified into similarities to diminish differences and decrease conflict and promote commonalities and oneness.

AFTER DEATH

Some humans have healed their abusive parent AFTER the parent's death. The parent stayed earth bound and hung around the abused ADULT child. The adult child then educated the parent about being a victim and then predator and how the cycle goes round and round. The adult child talks aloud to the parent, reads books, shows films and generally educates the parent of the dynamics of childhood sexual abuse and violence. When you think they understand and are aware of the damage they caused offer to take them to the bridge of flowers and cross them over. Have them put their hand in yours and hand them off to the angels on the bridge. Yes it all happens in your imagination.

The BRIDGE of FLOWERS is a point of separation from the near realms and the lower negative vibration INTO a positive range of emotions and the angelic realms. When a soul leaves their biology to get help and guidance they can go to the bridge of flowers where the angels meet and greet the soul to help it adjust to the transition and a higher vibrational level. They also help the soul process new awareness. Of those trying to get to the bridge after death only twenty percent arrive and the other eighty percent get lost in the near realms and take another body without increasing their wisdom or vibration generally. Humans can take souls directly to the bridge of flowers so they do not get side tracked or lost in the near realms.

Awareness of WHAT is TRUE heals you dead or alive.

Demonsare entities or relatives without biology and have very little if any light. As all dark does they blame and judge and live to punish anyone they can and siphon their energy. They have an inability to take responsibility for themselves, their behavior and their thoughts. They take great delight in tormenting those with biologies and light energy, especially the next generation in the bloodline. They feel entitled like all darkness does. Dark **truths** are ALWAYS unconscious. They do not own or take responsibility for the world they CREATED for them self. Dark is not capable of love and unconditional love is beyond their awareness. They see them self as the long-suffering victim.

Darkness is dangerous to spend time with because being FAIR, equitable or compassionate is not in their bag of tricks. They WILL siphon your energy, money and your self-esteem. Dark is ALWAYS mean spirited and most dark energy is ignorant of universal law or they twist it's meaning like the illuminati does to steal your energy.

Doing nothing is a choice to surrender to the largest bully.

Ask your invisible aspects if demons ever control your behavior, yes or no?

Ask which relative and for what percent of the time? Can you please have a slide or feeling show?

We are on a planet of free will so our invisible aspects rescuing us is considered force and interference. The RULES of this earth game is you have the tools to be your own superhero. No one is allowed to do anything FOR you. This is your test ALONE in spirituality. All DEMONS and their minions are generated by HUMAN consciousness. Dwell in darkness and you live in darkness.

Being in dark company makes you darker and might convince you that they DO have your soul. When we feel powerless we may well behave like we are in alignment with darkness or Satan making many little dark choices because the little human believe that light is too hard to attain and the light will reject you anyway so why bother. That is NOT a universal truth, it happens to be only a truth for the little human living on earth having a free will experience on behalf of their soul.

Many families have a family demon or more, that can go way back in the DNA line to Atlantis or hundreds of years back. An ancestor could have struck a deal with the devil, demon or any other kind of darkness on this planet, as there are many varieties of dark behavior to pick from. The ancestor was feeling insecure or inadequate so they invited a demon in to increase their HUMAN power, control or vengeance. The demon says, OH YES I can get that for you. Remember dark always lies.

The demon has an infinite life span and memory.

The demon now has been INVITED INTO the family and is dancing around rubbing its hands with glee very ready and able to help you sabotage yourself and all others that trust and depend on you. The demon now has access to all future generations and is CREATING and demonstrating a template of darkness and negativity for family members to follow forever, a family tradition of dysfunction, dependence and a need for others to care for you and enable you.

If you are not healing you have not reached the truth yet. Awareness that you have been abused or traumatized only comes in when you are able to have a supportive, balanced listener to share that information with.

Your invisible aspects want to be your listener.

You need help to make sense of what took place.

The biology does NOT forget the abuse. The trauma and abuse is stored in the biology. Body pain, blockages, density and disease must be acknowledged before it will leave. Keep suppressing your awareness, and your body will create headaches, heart problems, and other physical maladies that will just seem to escalate creating more problems JUST to gain your FULL attention. You will come into the next life with the same challenges you have not resoled in this life.

Even if you are a predator now you WERE A VICTIM FIRST. Your memory and feeling of just how painful that was, will give you the compassion for yourself and your victims to keep you from future victimizing.

The child victim ALWAYS feels guilty and responsible for CAUSING the predator to do what they did. The child ALWAYS blames itself. When a child is used sexually, they are told in many different ways it is THEIR fault and they believe that, they OWN ALL THE BLAME and they are never able to figure out why there is no love?

All judgment comes from FEAR children are full of fear. The fear that something is wrong with them or the adults wouldn't treat the child like they do. The predator or abuser projects onto the victim what they need to heal in them self.

Ask you invisible aspects what is true for you.

Chapter 5
TRAUMA or COMPASSION

Mindless violent sexual domination, drugging, electric shock and physical control of an infant is not compassion. Abusive, dissociated and dysfunctional mothers around the world that have female children HATE them and physically torture them and abandon them emotionally and frequently physically. These moms hate especially the female child because she knows the father will probably be the infant's first handler and violently rape the infant daily as "training" to be a child sexual slave. Mum is VERY angry at the awareness that she has lost her husbands "programmed love" to her daughter. Psychologically that is so twisted I do not know where to start making sense of it other than to say it does not make any logical sense. The children are the only ones that mom feels SAFE venting on.

Infants and small children generally don't fight back. She is angry about her abuses and trapped because she doesn't know how to change or get out of her situation when she is in present time. That only happens for a few minutes once in a while.

MOM

Accept the reality that mom is dangerous ESPECIALLY to her children, her grand children and any child she can lay her hands on. She will dissociate and do cruel things. For example after delivering her child and while still in the hospital one mother broke the large toe of another infant she knew nothing about. It took the doctor a long time to figure out what the baby was crying about. Illuminati mothers are very dark scary people home alone with an infant or two.

Boy babies have similar carefully crafted painful experiences. Infant children are subjected to cruel fingers, nails, teeth, cigarettes, genital torture or alligator clips, straps whips, dildos, electric shock and endless drugging. Some mothers kick the crawling infant around like a football for mom's tension relief.

Mom siphons the child's light and if you are wise you will give her back the dark you carry for her and just WALK AWAY.

Do the same for your father or any of your dark siblings or relatives. They are on their OWN path of many small dark choices, you need to allow that and it will raise YOUR vibration. Try to rescue them and you both get darker. Try to "play" the dark and you join them.

Ask your invisible aspects what percent light your mom has?

Ask your invisible aspects what percent light your dad has? Now you know which MIGHT be safer of the two to deal with. The wisest course and most aligned with the legion of light and universal law is to just walk away from them all and lean into your invisible aspects.

Ask for slide shows of her or his treatment of you as an infant.

NONE of the active illuminati members or any of abused, dissociated and dysfunctional mothers and fathers around the world possesses the capacity to NURTURE, support or PROTECT their children. They are DANGEROUS to children and them self. They were unable to protect themselves.

They have never nurtured themselves so they have NEVER nurtured a child.

Seriously abused children find being an adult of any age an overwhelming challenge. Their main concern throughout childhood was surviving ONE more TRAUMA from the people they depended on for their existence, nurturing, guidance and survival. There was NO TIME to develop the basic life skills or concentrate on higher-level knowledge and thought gathering at school. Like integrating information from your experiences and how to be functional enough to hold a job or fit in with the rest of society.

Some abused children have an alternate personality that can function at school or work but that is all they can do. For example I had one student with three alters that I saw. Only one of the alternate personalities knew how to read and write. The alternate personality that could read and write was only out about a fourth of the time at school. That didn't leave much to work with academically.

Another very common example is that many illuminati slaves perform their jobs in society robotically and well enough to get paid. BUT there is no alternate personality or energy left for when they are off work. There is no energy or desire to take care of daily tasks like cleaning, cooking, organizing, compassionate childcare or increasing knowledge or awareness. THERE IS yelling, hitting, abuse "hanging out" and compulsive distractions.

INTIMACY with another human OR being compassionate with the self OR staying in present time are not things the illuminati slave or abused children have skill or experience with. The adult abused child finds it real HARD to know how to function in the world EXCEPT when an alter takes over and follows orders.

Other people in the life of an abused child or adult take TURNS using and abusing them. The illuminati slave is programmed to comply and always do what others want or they might get PUNISHED. So when interacting with them and you are a slave also you will trigger each other's programs.

When there is one illuminati slave and one that isn't, the one that isn't will experience mostly passive-aggressive abuse. There is a long list of things they just NEVER do and had no intention of doing in spite of what they told you. A slave lies and goes for the truth as a last resort. Fear of further abuse and delusions of EARNING love runs their life. As all cult children must set aside their emotional growth and normal development because the cult has no use for that and it would interfere with the slaves programming.

"Programmed people" and anyone living in fear are unable to collect data from their life experiences, and PROCESS that data into a workable plan to change their behavior and thoughts. Because each alter or dissociated part keeps experiencing the same thing over and over and does not remember how the experience started, proceeded or ended. Just ONE alternate personality cannot collect ENOUGH information to understand what happens OVER and over again. One alternate personality can never grasp the larger picture.

To grasp the big picture you NEED to stop dissociating so you can see what the group of alters does to complete a task. First you get triggered you dissociate and change alternate personalities. The next alter may get dressed in a red dress. The handlers take you to a place. What the person "says" or the "way they touch you," brings up the alter that gives a message it got earlier. Another alternate personality records the answer even with the exact voice inflection. Then a whole set of alters allow and pretend to enjoy violent sex with one or many. The current handler takes you some place private or to the person that will get the answer to your message that your alter recorded mentally. A little electric shock and that alternate personality repeats the massage EXACTLY as it was given. Then a handler erases what the alternate personalities know. More electric shock and you are taken home to your handler parents or spouse.

Elementary and high school students carry many of these messages, as most of these people that get and give messages, both male and female are pedophiles. These students generally have a high absentee rate from school. They are exhausted when they wake up having no idea they ever left home.

This is the way our top political leaders, the military and drug dealers and Illuminati elite communicates secretly and send messages. Illuminati slaves do it all the time and have no idea what they have done. If they remembered any of it and told someone would they be believed? If they reported anything they would be in for more punishment. The human robot not being aware is a way to survive.

Ask your invisible aspects for a slide show about what your biology actually DOES that you are not consciously aware of.

MORE EXAMPLES

An example of a slave functioning in what we call the real world.

Tom ripped Sarah off the 1st, 2nd and 3rd time she interacted with him. If she didn't dissociate each time and change alternate personalities she would know he would probably rip her off a 4 and 5 time they interact. But Sarah NEVER gets it. The cult or fearful abused child never sees that. Each interaction with Tom is the first time or a "fresh start" for Sarah and she wants him to like her. The dissociation and emotional immaturity is what gets Sarah into the same cycle of self-defeating behavior over and over again. This cycle of blind trust, dissociation and wanting to be liked goes on in ALL her relationships, even in business. Sarah has no awareness of repeated experiences that create the same outcome almost every time. She is ALWAYS surprised when she hasn't been treated fairly or gets ripped off.

Another example is that Kim gets raped or has sex every time he meets someone. This is also true for children suffering disorganized abuse. The abused child and adult have no BOUNDARIES and never say NO to avoid more abuse. There is a LACK of boundaries found in many dysfunctional families. Does Kim get raped or triggered or dissociates and gets taken advantage of, only Kim might know if he stayed in present time long enough to figure it out.

When you don't remember or CANNOT track the entire event from beginning until the end you have dissociated and lost YOUR control and CLARITY of the situation and what happened. People say Kim wanted it to happen because he LET the same thing happen to him over and over again. That might not be true.

Pick something that confuses you and ask your invisible aspects for a slideshow of the entire event. Getting clarity about what REALLY happened is VERY helpful and healing but you must stay in present time.

The abused know they have NO rights or boundaries and anyone can do to them what they want to do. Any child or mentally challenged or abused individual lack awareness of basic logic or will deny it because they are always fearful and guilty of not being worthy so they blindly accept that whatever another person says. They are convinced others know more and are wiser. More faulty reasoning from the abused is "if I offer compassion to darkness" they will return LOVE to me. They try that all the time and always get the same result. The abused child does not realize that when you offer compassion to the very dark they read that as you are WEAK and EASY to take advantage of and they DO. The dark individual or group is NOT CAPABLE of love and compassion they read love and compassion as weakness, an "easy mark" they must take advantage of.

None of what is characteristic of females is valued by the illuminati. Feminine energy is creativity, nurturing, warmth or understanding and has no value to the illuminati. They enjoy ritual, hierarchy and "King of the Hill" force and servants. Their favorite "role playing game" is "survival" and "I kill you" and they do it all in the name of their god Satan. Just like all the humans that go to war to force their religious beliefs on each other. Low-level dark gods are the ones that take your free will, creativity and ability to THINK for yourself away so you are easily controlled.

Sometimes trainers or controllers question what "they call a demonic entity" called the HIDDEN OBSERVER to find out things about an illuminati slave and their behavior and thoughts. The cult is actually spying on you by questioning YOUR invisible aspects about you.

Ask your invisible aspects if they have been questioned about you yes or no? Ask about what and can I please have a slide show.

Know that the angelic realms are in alignment with the universal laws.

There are no secrets in higher vibrations. When your higher vibrational aspects are asked questions they will honestly TELL what they know when asked. You can tell your invisible aspects to keep things a secret about you and when asked they will not share with lower dimensions or vibrations because they do not operate within universal law.

Scientology calls your invisible aspects the "file clerk." The file clerk is your invisible aspects telling you "about you" and you can do it for free, at no cost.

The universal law of **ACTION** means you must ACT first in order for something you want to start moving in the direction you want it to move. Then your invisible aspects will co-create the action with you and others join in after you make the first move or many little moves to get things rolling and prove your commitment and intent to move forward.

The universal law of **BALANCE** is to maintain order and harmony within the divine universe. Accept and OWN the human traits you have in the now moment. Accept and own the things and awareness your invisible aspects present to you. Each entity makes the CHOICE to exist. When those choices are made in synchronicity with the flow of other entities and EVENTS balance is maintained. Humans are 10% of their soul and we are balancing spiritual energy with physical matter. For every action there is a reaction. You may not know what the reaction is but there is one some place. Nothing happens the way you expect it to. BUT you NEED to notice it when it does happen and take advantage of their expert help.

Some humans have the mistaken belief that victimhood and suffering makes them more spiritual but the OPPOSITE is true. When you live in the victimhood and suffering cycle you are actually rejecting your divine aspects and the soul tends to go away until you figure things out. Victimhood is not a desirable place to live because of the low vibration it has.

ALIEN Programming has blue beams of light as a hypnotic induction for slaves who are given the cover story of being abducted by aliens. The All-Seeing Eye is used to represent the planet Sirius important to the Hermetic magicians. Satan is said to come from Draco or Sirius the Dog Star Canis Major. Sirius may represent the creator of the systems when the programmer is steeped in Masonic philosophy. A sickle may represent the Garden of Eden story for some victims of this kind of programming.

Illuminati slaves are feed with so many lies. Whatever you believe you are given something that counters it. It is all about extreme duality. Rise above and out of all that contrast by communing with your invisible aspects.

Ask your invisible aspects if you have had alien programming?

PSYCHIC TRAINING

You say that you have always known what others feel or think. Were you born into the illuminati cult and programmed?

Ask your invisible aspects, yes or no?

Roughly a third of babies born on earth are born into satanic cults and are programmed and traumatized from before and after birth. Programming or their stimulus-response learning is generally terrorizing someone into such a state of fear and trauma his or her awareness goes to another dimension or someplace else while the biology is being traumatized and forced by the bully or did you call your abuser mom, dad or grandparent. Survival of these endless traumas becomes the infants MAIN concern or they just go into the fetal position and die physically. When the biology keeps living the psyche or soul is seriously wounded and waits until the human starts to raise its vibration enough to get away from the abuse by leaving it or home and or the illuminati cult.

From the spiritual point of perception YOU CHOSE to be born to very wounded robotic cruel parents for a spiritual reason. Our sexual energy is a strong psychic energy that is difficult to disconnect from. Energetic sexual abuse, without physical touch is being seductive and treating the child or adult as a sexual object without physically touching but the interaction has a sexual flavor, PROMISE, or flirting, and teasing masquerading as compassion. Seductive energy is very confusing to a child that is 100% dependent on another to stay alive and doesn't know what is real. Sexual energy is the most conflictual, anxiety provoking CONSUMING addiction there is amongst the dark. They use sexual energy as a means of distraction, control, manipulation and a base twisted kind of satisfaction.

Ask your invisible aspects why you chose that?

Your RESPONSE to what happened to you in that family or group is what determines your spiritual growth. Are you aligning with universal law and your light invisible aspects or is your choice to stay with darkness and negativity waiting to be rescued by any superhero?

Of all the babies "jumped in" to the illuminati gang at birth 10% of the satanic ritually abused infants are programmed in their first years to FOCUS on developing their psychic abilities. It would be likely that one of the genetic parents excelled in psychic skills also. These toddlers at 2 to 3 years of age start working for their handlers and keep on working for them until they CONSCIOUSLY decide to STOP or die. They can scan a room, country or plant for the group awareness or an individual awareness and report their findings back to the handler. Psychic toddlers are opened to the universe and receive uncensored information easily. Because they are slaves, like all the other slaves their energy base is not grounded anyplace. They are scattered or "buttered all over the universe."

A normal toddler isn't very grounded either.

The psychic toddler will have done remote viewing, information gathering, found portals, psychically read other cult members and everyone else. In doing that they have left "aspects" of them self scattered all over the universe. They are CONFUSED about who they really are and where they start and end.

They compulsively reach for the clarity their handlers do not want them to have and are unable to give. The psychic and empathic toddlers along with all the other BASIC programming they get are not able to discern their own feelings or thoughts from all the other things they feel, see and read. They do not understand what is their OWN feeling and NEEDS or what is someone else's need or want. The child or adult illuminati psychic or empathic doesn't know where THEY stop and OTHER entities or events begin. Most of what they see and feel is pain, suffering and confusion because that is what is present here on earth. There is a great deal of darkness especially in the illuminati.

Children blame them self and grow up to be adults that still blame them self when things go wrong in their life. They feel GUILTY, angry and trapped and as long as they stay with the illuminati as an active cult member and stay in contact with abusive family members or abusive relatives, jobs, religions, organizations or dark friends they will stay stuck.

GUILT is a type of paralysis that arises when the mind holds opposing desires equally matched in intensity. To stay with the only family or spouse they have ever known or walk away? Guilt is a useless human emotion that destroys self-image, self-esteem and positive expression. Guilty people give pieces of them self away to those they are talked into feeling guilty about. Guilt and punishment are tools of the dark to control you and have NO spiritual value or wisdom at all.

COMPROMISE is a settlement in which two or more sides agree to accept LESS. Some humans compromise so much of their ENERGY and MIND that they have lost WHO they are. When they doubt them self they become fragmented, fearful and rather STUBBORN.

COMPETITION tethers you to your FEAR. Competition can never be a win-win-win.

COMPLIANCE is the easiest way to steal another's energy. The energy stealing crosses into the NEXT lifetime and in-between each lifetime setting up a cycle of hopelessness in its victims. It bleeds into ones SOUL energy and is a way to enslave or entrap the soul and create wicked kar-mic energies between two or more individuals. The illuminati slave is in danger of their soul turning dark.

The psychically programmed child and adult are gener-ally the ones most likely to break their programming enough to leave the cult and biological family, which is what needs to be done to heal and grow lighter. Also the abused child needs to leave the biological family and clan and or the abuser to heal and grow lighter.

An example of breaking your own programming is Jane. The family members raised her with all the basic program-ming, raping and at 4 years of age she had enough "train-ing" at home. Being psychic she could read their nasty dark thoughts. She was done with living. She frequently tried to commit suicide by running away on her tricycle or climbing trees or standing in the bullpen provoking the bull.

At twelve years of age, she and her mother cared for her satanic grandpa that was dying. Grandpa felt sexual lust for the 12 year old, which is typical in pedophiles and Satanists. The mother was EXCEEDINGLY jealous and felt betrayed by her daughter. Mom thought she had EARNED the right to have "the love" of grandpa. Mom blamed and hated her daughter. Mom HATED her daughter intensely. The daughter read her mind. The daughter was so upset by mom's hate and rejection that the child decided at that time to STOP feeling or reading what any human felt or thought ANYMORE. She broke her own programming at age 12.

An example of an empathic child enjoying her creativity, drawing and play that gave her great joy. The caretaker got jealous and angry with the empathic child enjoying itself. The child assumes they are wrong to enjoy themselves and stifles the creativity and much of her personality to please the care-taker. That compromise creates a miserable child and adult.

THETA Programming is PSYCHIC warfare. The illuminati train their slaves to use their psychic powers to kill someone psychically from a distance by poking holes in their auric fields. There are even weapon systems that operate on the power of the mind and whose lethal capacity has already been demonstrated. Many of the military are young men and women of the Illuminati. Some have been seen at NORAD, in Colorado, which helps confirm that Theta model slaves are being employed to bring in the Anti-Christ, the large white dragon with blue eyes of a very low vibration or "El" the god of Saturn and supreme deity represented by a black cube.

TWISTED SPIRITUALITY

SPIRITUAL Programmingincludes being forced to memorize rituals and the "Book of Illumination" and other cult beliefs. This happens to children from infancy on. Classes and training sessions on rituals and spiritual worship to the particular guardian deity of your group like Moloch, Ashtaroth, Baal, Enokkim are the demons commonly worshipped. The child is forced to participate in sacrifices and blood baptism and forced to take the heart or other internal organs out of the sacrificed and eat them. The drugged and hypnotized child has the hands of the leader placed on the child's head while INVOKING demonic entities to enter the child's biology.

For the RESUSCITATION ritual the child is heavily drugged and shocked or tortured until their HEART stops beating. Then the head priest will resuscitate the child with drugs, CPR and incantations. When the child comes back or is resuscitated they are told that they were brought back to life by the demonic entity the group worships and now the child owes their life to that entity.

Sometimes the carcass of a large animal like a cow or horse is opened up and the child is placed in there for a day or more so it can be REBORN into Satan's legions. Sometimes the child dies, but if they live they are told the demon saved them.

Jewel programming will often have demons loyal to the generational family spirits or FAMILY JEWELS layered in. The lie is that if you accept the dark protector you won't be hurt anymore.

Ask your invisible aspects if you have had spiritual programming? Can you have a slide show of your earliest spiritual programming?

One of the illuminati spiritual teachings is the **BOOK of PHERYLLT.** This book is a Druidic book of rituals or the Illuminati's brand of Druidism. Visualization and magic is used to open the portals of the 4 basic elements air, water, earth, and fire to control events the Satanists want control of. The Illuminati forces the two-year-old child to carry alters for Druidism, Christianity and Satanism and possibly others. When the illuminati slave places their faith in a "human or reptilian" created faith or belief systems they WAIT to be SAVED.

Waiting to be saved means you have not awakened to the legion of light and universal law that says you must save YOUR SELF.

Illuminati spiritual training is also found in **JESUIT and CATHOLIC Programming** the Jesuit branch of the Illuminati placed tattoos on their mind-controlled slaves consisting of the sacred heart with a rose and a dagger on the left hand in the 1940's. The Jesuits have discontinued the practice of tattooing their slaves.

ENTER INTER INNER dimension two is a standard Jesuit infinity program. 2 is a sacred voodoo number. The Pontiff or the pope is a DEMON and alter placed in the Jesuit systems.

The Alice In Wonderland programming themes use "air-water programs" and have mirror programs. The Illuminati, the CIA, NASA and the Jesuits like the idea of a MIRROR WORLD that is a reversal of our world. In the "reverse mirror world" a slave can enter into timelessness or "interdimensional time travel." This mirror programming is in locations around the America, like the Magic Time Machine restaurants in San Antonio and Dallas, TX where mirrors are placed on doors, ceilings, walls, and restrooms. The handler may tell the slave, "LOSE YOURSELF IN THE INFINITY MIRRORS." When programming in programs, many types of images are used. The Jesuits and the Catholic churches are active in programming in Germany and use obedience confession and self-criticism. Positive experiences are used to increase self worth like you are growing stronger and stronger.

The Jesuits developed torture to a fine art during the inquisition and brought that expertise to the illuminati Monarch Programming started before birth. The Jesuits brag that they can convince adults to do anything via torture.

"Baby's breathe" and the black rose has to do with death and WHITE ROSE are codes and triggers used in Jesuit mind control. Mafia uses the black rose and was used by George Bush the drug kingpin for the Illuminati. When the Catholic Priest does the hand signal genuflection it has the second meaning of north, south, east and west as in the Book of Pheryllt.

Ask your invisible aspects if you have mirror programming? Ask for a slide show of the program.

The **RITE to REMAIN SILENTProgramming** is a satanic reversal of the Catholic Mass or the Black Mass with the Black Mary. The VOW OF SILENCE is a keep quiet program activated by "The walls have ears and the plants have eyes." It is explained to the victim that the seashells and plants have the ability to hear and a sensitive occultist or programmer can psychically pick up what the plants and seashells hear. "MAINTAIN IT" is a command to maintain the Vow of Silence. "MAINTAIN IT and LISTEN" is a command to keep silent and listen to the command that is coming up soon.

Programmers make many mistakes and a lot of experimenting goes on all the time a Programming FAILURE or PFS. Trainers like to tell their subjects that they are experiments even when they aren't for several reasons:

1. It creates immense fear and helplessness in the subject.

2. It devalues the person that THINKS that all they are is an experiment and they give up hope.

3. It gives the trainer added power because they are the one who can start or stop the EXPERIMENT.

When trainers really do experiments the subject is never told. The fear is that it could interfere with the drug effects and skew the results.

HISTORICALLY

SLAVE BANDS are what scientists came up with in Atlantis to create slaves. They put a metal band around the slave's head and NAILED it into their skull. They told the human it was their CROWN. The band acted as a DISRUPTER of the electrical system like a cattle prod disrupts cattle from the direction they want to go. The band prevented clear thought and even being able to think. This thought disruption put the human into fear and DEPENDENCY just like the current illuminati slave or abused child is kept in fear and dependency needing someone to do their thinking for them all the time to avoid more punishment and suffering.

The band was given to 50% of the population IN Atlantis. Those still being affected by those bands are 50% of the population on earth living today and many are in America. The individuals that put these mind control bands on other humans are suffering the same fate during this lifetime as the slaves suffered then. Between lives the suffering gets even greater for the slave so they keep coming back into biology to relieve the suffering.

Ask your invisible aspects if you ever wore a slave band during Atlantis?

Ask your invisible aspects if you ever put slave bands on people during Atlantis?

Are you currently wearing a slave band on and astral body?

VLAD the IMPALER or DRACULA comes from the royal reptilian Illuminati bloodlines. Every part ofthe world and era of history has legends of VAMPIRES that feed off people's energy and blood. Dracula contains all the familiar vampire themes he is called COUNT and shapeshifts. He ate among the dead bodies, dipping his bread in their blood. Vlad the Impaler slaughtered tens of thousands of people and impaled many of them on STAKES.Thenot too sharp stake was oiled and SLOWLY forced into the body. VLAD didn't want the victim dyingtoo quickly from shock.

Impalement takes hours or days to kill. Infants were often impaled on the stake forced through their mothers' chests, sometimes hung upside down on the stake. Dracula had thestakes arranged in various geometric patterns, mostly concentric circles. Theheight of the spear indicated the rank of the victim. Impalement was Dracula's favorite but by no means his only method of inflictingunimaginable HORROR and suffering. Vlad was the son of Vlad Dracul, who was initiated into the ancient Order of the Dragon by theHoly Roman Emperor in 1431. The ancient Order of theDragon began in Egypt and is currently practiced by the mother of King George VI and grandmother to the present Elizabeth II in England.

The illuminati is ever present.

Chapter 6
FREQUENCY SORTING

Key to illuminati programming is that the slave never has conscious awareness or control of what they do. They do have the "illusion of deciding" what they want to do all the time.

Close to a third of the earth's population were CO-VERTLY raised to be "compliant illuminati mind-controlled slaves" designed to help bring in the New World Order and New World Religion. The slave being conscious would get in the way of the illuminati's smooth running dark and perverse operation, which they are VERY proud of. They think humans are a lower, less evolved form of life to be used anyway they want to use us.

The illuminati were first to inhabit earth and created the various religions on roughly the same theme. ALL the religions tell the same stories we find in the bible and other religious texts. The stories are all rewrites of your basic "Satan" from Draco or "EL" from Saturn that are designed to glorify and empower the little human or reptilian. They all carry the same message of "follow this deity" or be punished or get killed or you will not be saved. This VERY common religious theme is a very low and dark vibration of control, force and manipulation.

All the religions claim to be doing "gods work" by going through the universe dominating and assimilating inferior creatures and slaves, like humans are said to be. Our earth religions think we need to take the "native" or "pagan" land, their natural resources and their money and force our "version of god," GUILT and control on them. I do not see any difference from what the reptilians do in the universe and what humans do here on earth. All the religions have created low vibrational "dark gods" for them selves and everyone else they can take something of value from.

All of "the low vibrational gods" take your free will and ability to choose and THINK for your self. They keep you focused and fearful with "fire and brimstone," or "sound and light shows" to keep your attention diverted OUTWARD.

The focus is to keep your "VEHICLE" or biology alive and amused to prevent you from seeing the larger picture of what is really true. Because our essence is infinite our vehicle or biology dying is not such a big deal. Our vehicles have died MANY times before while our essence remains as ever.

If your soul goes darker because the human is "drunk with the power of their vehicle" and "little human gods" that is a VERY sad dark story.

THAT is NOT the way of it in higher vibrations.

When YOU have diverted YOU and your awareness with distractions from your inner alignment with your invisible aspects, universal law and the legion of light your invisible aspects can't channel universal energy to you. Without that energy the vehicle or biology starts to die unless you can siphon energy / light from others that carry energy / light. In fact that is exactly what the dark gods and the illuminati are doing all the time.

When darkness feeds on each other and there is no light energy left to siphon, the biology and essence or soul start disintegrating into basic elements and becomes space dust. This can take a long time and many others may go dark and die in the process. Their many small negative choices and vampirism ways fail to produce the light energy to be infinite. That's how the legion of light gives free will. Go lighter or fall into your atomic structure and be recycled.

This era of giving humans experiences with matter has ended and is over. Our invisible aspects are trying hard to get "their human aspect" sorted out and in alignment with the photon belt and the higher vibration we are going through for the next 2,000 years, to complete the FREQUENCY sorting of humans and others on earth. The higher vibrating are moving into oneness and the lower vibrating are in the process of being relocated for another 26,000-year cycle of duality and lessons or falling into their atomic structure.

Our invisible aspects are trying to "awaken" and raise the vibration of their humans as fast and as much as they can. They really want those with light, trapped in the illuminati "sound and light show" to WAKE UP and hear the greater range of frequencies coming from different dimensions.

TO HEAL and GUIDE YOU

Your invisible aspects have created bundles of aware-ness on a theme of the things you need to heal. Our invisible aspects are giving their humans SLIDE SHOWS of what was true for the human. Your awareness and acceptance of what is TRUE in your past will heal you. PLEASE No more pretty stories or "pleasing others" or "compromising" just to keep the biology alive.

The **SLIDE SHOWS** are presented to the minds eye when you are asleep or awake. When your invisible aspects give you a vision or feeling from your childhood or concur-rent life there is something for you to SEE and OWN to increase your spiritual wisdom. The slide show may be your WOUNDS on the same theme in this and concurrent lives. The theme could be a behavior pattern you have repeated over and over you need to understand and own. Themes like you having a closed heart in many life times. OR the many times your heart was closed in this life. Have you lived your life waiting for another to PROVE they love you before you even consider returning a bit of caring or love? That is not the way of higher vibrations.

When your invisible aspects think you are ready they will bring you a bundle and another bundle to help you release more duality by experiencing ONE LAST time what your beliefs and creations brought you. Frequently you are not even aware you had an issue with what they present OR you were sure you already handled that issue, years ago. You probably did BUT there is a particular aspect or perception they want you to REVISIT and feel, all on the same chain all at the same time.

When your fear is one of being abandoned you close your heart to avoid pain. Living in a low vibration as we do there is no way to avoid pain consider embracing the pain and move through it as fast as you can. People die and we feel abandoned or rejected. Injustice or cruelty of others is the way of duality, accept that reality and give thanks to your biology for being in service to you.

For example you lost a relationship or house because they no longer served your needs. You were so attached to the thing or the caretaking it prevented your spiritual growth. Your attachment fostered the illusion of safety and control. See the larger picture BEFORE raising your vibration another notch.

Possibly you have a gift you withheld because people haven't been NICE to you and you have upset yourself about that. You brought that in from your last life unresolved. When you want to know about it YOU ask your entourage or invisible aspects to give you a slide show with feelings of what is TRUE to clear up YOUR confusion or density or lack of clarity. They can give you a show or information about how another in your experience really FELT and thought. Instead of you guessing, what they thought or felt.

FEELING SLIDE SHOWis when your invisible aspects give you a feeling BUNDLE that stays with you that has nothing to do with present time. For example, the feeling of being tired or sick was that how you felt as a child? Did your stomach stay upset all the time? The feeling will stay with you until you are AWARE and own that was how you REALLY felt. After you OWN that feeling you will get a 2nd and 3rd feeling to accept and own as yours.

Ask your invisible aspects anything else you may want to know. They can share everyone else's feelings involved with YOUR feeling experience. These feelings are given by your invisible aspects to HELP release your pockets of density or TENSION you have held in your biology. The physical tension anchors in the biology and DNA. Having a realistic point of perception and FEELING of your childhood or concurrent lives allows you to come to some resolution and release.

ENTRAINMENT vs. PROGRAMMING

The universal law of **ENTRAINMENT** REQUIRES that two resonances or vibrations or humans existing in the same location MUST adjust and combine to have a single resonance. Predators and victims do that all the time and that is why they are able to read each other's thoughts and FEELINGS and know what the other plans to do next. But some read the thought, get horrified and dissociate. As long as they are dissociated they have no control and they ALLOW the predator to do as they wish.

Entrainment is a locking onto each other, a meeting in the middle. In physics it is IONIC or atomic BONDING formed by the attraction of two oppositely charged ions or atoms. When we can radiate light ions from the heart chakra and another entity is open to receive them there is an electrostatic bonding. The two or more become entrained. They feel and are consciously aware of what the other is feeling, thinking and planning to do. As the example above the bonding can also be for a dark reason UNTIL the point of dissociation. Then the bonding or entrainment is over and you move into programming.

PROGRAMMING is a stimulus-response or conditioning or associative learning sequence. A significant stimulus evokes a REFLEXIVE response. For example smelling something cooking you like to eat starts the saliva in your mouth flowing.

When reading the intention of your predator evokes the reflexive response of dissociation you are unable to change the outcome until you get back in the biology and stay in the now moment. It is always your choice. IF one decides to dissociate there is only one human vibration and no one to entrain with. If one decides to dissociate there is no one home to interact with and the bully does as they wish.

You allowed the bully to control you by default. You failed to stand in your truth or consciously walk away. You can't walk away if you are denying what is true.

SHARED SYMPTOMS

Most common symptoms of those who have been programmed before and after their birth are EXTREMELY low self-worth or self-esteem. They are frequently depressed and or suicidal. Some have obsessive-compulsive disorder. They vomit to expel drugs or are bulimic to expel emotional upset. All are sexually addicted and some fight it successfully. The low level vibration of the lower chakras "sexual addiction" is what the illuminati want along with promiscuity, violence and all the guilt and fear that goes with that.

Gender Identity Disorder GID, issues are common because the illuminati treat both sexes the same way regardless of their sexual organs. The child and adult do not feel a strong identification with either sex. Females get a bit more abuse because they were born to serve and are needed as breeders. BUT Illuminati can clone themselves so females are not that important except for DNA experimentation, to create more food, more slaves and be violently raped.

All mind-control slaves share POST TRAUMATIC STRESS DISORDER or PTSD. Slaves are full of shattered hurting alters and the slave is UNAWARE of them all collectively and generally is in denial about any pain. Self-punishment and social withdrawal are natural symptoms of PTSD and programmed slaves.

Programmers enhance the low level painful emotions into the alter systems because they all work to the advantage of the trainer. Different alters end up holding the AN-GER, fear, social withdrawal, GUILT, promiscuity and DE-SIRE for self inflicted punishment. Illuminati slaves tend to be VERY self-absorbed judging, blaming and criticizing the self in endless loops that take them NO PLACE. Just as all small wounded children are angry frustrated and suffering.

These negative and self-destructive feelings are held in check and balanced by other parts of the programming and become part of the personality. When the slave considers leaving the illuminati, the control systems of fear, negativity and suicide come forward to keep the slave trapped. Some alters even call or tell the handlers that the slave is trying to leave.

When you DISSOCIATE you are powerless.

When a slave or traumatized individual feels SAFE, then the alternate personalities can start to integrate them self. During danger, an intricate interaction of biological, and nervous system reactions occurs. This interaction causes the muscles to contract to protect the organism from harm or death. Once the danger has subsided the body is designed to SHAKE OUT excessive muscular tension. We have deadened this shaking mechanism from the fight or flight muscle system and they are the only ones that connect the back, pelvis and legs and as they relax the natural shaking of the body reverberates throughout the entire biology looking for tension to dissolving it in a natural way.

Masochism or self-hate is thoughts, feelings and judgments that loop over and over in the brain. The child was treated badly and ASSUMES they did something wrong and need to be punished. The child never considers that they were born into endless darkness and dark does what it always does. Have your awareness and leave that vibration.

The universal law of **ATTRACTION** says the thoughts and emotions of the little human create a vibrational energy consciously or unconsciously that emanates from us and attracts like energy. The universe does not care if your emanations are real or IMAGINED, negative or positive. It simply reflects with CLARITY and TRUTH what is held in your energy field. Moving to the larger realities and truths enable us to release our rage, anger and frustration. The human is a temporary vehicle and was never designed to RULE. We are here to experience.

Self-love is acceptance and approval of what is in the NOW moment.

The universal law of **CAUSE and EFFECT or RE-CIPROCAL action** is that nothing happens by CHANCE or outside of universal laws. Every action has a reaction or consequence. You get back what you give ALL the TIME so be conscious of your emanations. IT IS NOT personal it is physics. Keep functioning at a survival level and you will keep attracting survival situations to master for your spiritual awareness on that level. Alignment WITH the universal laws will raise your vibration OUT of the illuminati low vibration.

TRIGGERS and FOCUS CHANGES

It is always helpful to be conscious of your TRIGGERS and FOCUS CHANGES so you can consciously DECIDE what you want to do. Triggers and focus changes can be words, ACTIONS, behaviors, SEEING a particular thing, a particular smell, sound, message or phone call and some get psychically contacted.

Ask your invisible aspects, which trigger you need to be conscious of the MOST. Ask if they will help you notice it when it happens? That way you can be in control of what you do.

Many popular movies, jingles and songs have triggers in them.

FOR EXAMPLE

A stare into your eyes" or a punch in stomach is a CUE to be submissive.

Some noises or car noises are a CUE to be fearful.

A hick-up can be a cue for you to go into CONFUSION.

"Lady in Red" is a trigger song to dance and get undressed.

Tiger is a trigger to go mentally foggy or into a state of hypnosis and act like a robot.

Kissing is a focus change to make you forget what happened just before the kiss.

Pain works well to change focus, pain in the head and stomach.

"You like it wild." You are a Wildcat, Tiger, and little girl, Bitch, Kiss me are all sexual triggers to become aroused and sexual in different ways.

Oh those eyes or you have beautiful eyes, you are so beautiful, he is so sexy ARE TRIGGARS to make the slave feel safe, trusting, loved and sexually excited.

SOME triggers start a series of actions. A SLAP is a trigger to close down the receiver program, to SHUT the file and open another program.

The VICTIM program is used to make the slave feel they have lost a love when all that has happened is handlers were switched. Stories you tell yourself about what has happened are YOU programming yourself.

Sexual behavior or lust programs can be started or intensified with a bite on the ear, a whisper of demeaning remarks in the ear or prolonged kisses.

You where beaten after the sexual abuse to forget what was really going on, all you remember is the physical abuse or the focus change, possibly a kiss.

A nurturing program is baby talk back and forth to your children and they baby talk back but no intimacy, caretaking or nurturing is really experienced by either end of the exchange.

For adults FAKING INTIMACY with "Hi Honey" and the response "Hi Baby" programming is two dissociated adults doing a stimulus-response act.

When your programming is triggered fight it by staying in present time. Cut into the dissociation and interrupt the darkness by bringing the human up to present time. Be proud of your self for staying in your biology in the now moment.

NEW WORLD ORDER and RELIGION

The illuminati had targeted the turn of the century to have their COVERT control of humans to become OVERT with the New World Order and New World Religion. They are like the serial killers that want you to know how very clever they were and now we can admire their handiwork and skill at terrorizing fetuses and small children. When that fails you get cannibalized for your fear energy, organs, hormones and blood.

We are so IMPRESSD that the illuminati can't deal with anyone that is conscious and has free will. They can never risk letting others know what they REALLY do. The illuminati want ROBOTS or clones they are not interested in individual thought or creativity or even change.

The issues and souls of Lemuria, Atlantis, the Roman Empire, Egypt and from other planets are back on earth running concurrently in the now moment for us to have a chance to make a DIFFERENT CHOICE, heal and REWRITE a lighter outcome for the human and its soul.

During Atlantis entities were able to reproduce within them self when they were **vibrating high enough** and had **enough wisdom** to have a child. Then came darkness, duality and the gender split. Men were given the power to exert their creativity and women were to hold and cultivate it in the holiest of unions rhythmically together. This was a rhythm that matched Gaia's own movements and brought alignment of humanity to Gaia and Gaia to the universe. The flows of Gaia and her plate tectonics to the water cycles are the ways our bodies are designed to move.

Darkness or the illuminati from Atlantis has DEGRADED this creative process down to their biological pieces or functions and taken the spiritual beauty out of reproduction. The humans allowed and some joined into the process. Semen is one of the most potent externalized fluids in our biology that the illuminati worship. They have taken the beauty and holiness out of creation and reduced it to cum!

PHILOSOPHY was originally conceived as the art of explaining the movements of the soul within the realm of matter and humans. Humans do not feel safe when they lose their high vibrations and lose the connection with their other 90%. The illuminati has worked hard to cut that connection and they succeed when you dissociate and leave the now moment.

The universal laws or HIGHER TRUTHS govern our reality and we are all under their influence. The more we understand about how the universal laws work in our life the easier it is to follow those truths UP to a higher vibration and freedom from the illuminati control, manipulation and force. Your invisible aspects have been waiting to assist you for a very long time, allow that to happen for you. On a planet of free will and duality you must ASK your invisible aspect for what you want one simple question at a time.

The Universal law of **FREE WILL** is divine will granting each entity the right to DIRECT and PURSUE his or her life so long as he or she does not violate the same right of others. A right that excludes the rights of others is NOT DIVINE.

The illuminati has managed to violate EVERYONES will, over and over again because we allowed it. If you wake up and evolve to higher vibrations they can play their game WITHOUT you. That can be your choice.

You will not be rescued.

You start fighting for your awareness NOW.

The Universal law of **LOVE** or **DIVINE ONENESS** is that everything is created from universal energy or unconditional love. All entities acceptWHAT IS. Free will does not come in PORTIONS you either have it or you do not have it. The Universe is a place of creation, experience and connection to everything else.

LEVELS of COMPASSION

The LEVEL of COMPASSION or awareness or light energy or vibration of the earth's population:

74% of earth's population is unconscious and NEGATIVE. They do not see the larger picture. The little human's capacity for compassion, vibration and light they carry correlate to each other. Your entourage, guides or angels reside in your auric field to help support and guide you in the dense energy of earth. Those carrying no light to 30% light are unconscious and vibrate too low for the invisible realm to assist so they wait for a higher vibration or more light in the human.

Level Below 0 to zero carries **no light to 15% light.** They act dead and operate in self-pity, blame, addictions and using other entities, humans and animals. They are easily possessed by any entity and the most likely possession is a dark ancestor or relative. The feelings and emotions of the little human that is unconscious include DENIAL, numbness, DISSOCIATED, grief and apathy. You would need to work yourself UP to level zero and RESENTMENT, anger, antagonism, blaming, acting out, SELF-hate and living life in anxiety and fear.

Level 0 carries **15 to 30%light.** They operate by abandoning their biology and their awareness. They feel betrayed by their biology and life. To cope they shut off their feelings, emotions and sensory awareness. They are unconscious and unaware.

21% of the population on earth is HALF CONSCIOUS. When you reach for higher thoughts little by little you go in and out of awareness and are a HALF CONSCIOUS human functioning emotionally in fear, indifference and boredom. You would need to work yourself UP to antagonism, anger contentment, hopefulness, and are able to consciously create some.

Level 1 carries **30 to 50% light.** They operate by being oppositional, angry, in pain and HATING. They are self absorbed, gossipy, fearful and frequently leaving their biology or living in past time. They are limited by their beliefs and fears and are irrational much of the time with a rather limited vision. They twist facts to defend their half conscious reality and truths. By the end of 2010 those below 50% light will move to another planet to continue the 3rd dimensional duality with a dark bias.

Level 2 carries **50 to 60% light.** They operate by being conventional, traditional and cautious they are 3/ 4 CONSCIOUS. They upset themselves when others do not follow the rules and are very proud of that. They DO tend to squelch the enthusiasm and inventiveness of others. They are followers, not adventurers and want to be entertained. They are cautious and want to be average and fit in. conscious.

4% of the population on earth is FULLY CONSCIOUS and reach for higher vibrational thoughts and are in sync with their invisible aspects and universal law.

Level 3 carries **60 to 70% light.** They are thriving, inquisitive, seeking and mostly conscious. At 60% and higher we are able to start loving and having compassion for our self. They function in awareness, interest, eagerness and creativity.

Level 4 carries **70 to 80% light.** They are eager, cheerful and enthusiastic. To move to the top of this band you would need to work yourself UP to JOY and passion as you merge with your soul. Consciousness determines your DESTINY not technology. With 70% light an entity or demon cannot posses your biology because you won't let it.

Of the little humans on earth only 2% have had a LIGHT lifetime.

1/2% or less humans are working on ASCENDING. For those wanting to merge with their soul / higher self and ascend they need to bring their compassion, light and awareness up to 80% so you are vibrating high enough to allow your higher self / soul to reside in your auric field.

Level 5 carries **80 to 90% light** andis called **IN and OUT** because 50% or less of the little human has merged with their higher self.

Level 6 carries **90 to 95% light** andis called **BALANCING** your biology and DNA. The human needs to show gratitude daily toward their biology for all its service to your essence. Be grateful to the biology for all the abuse you have experienced especially in childhood and managed to stay alive and functioning because of its innate intelligence and willingness to work with you in this density. The reconnecting of your strands of DNA into loops and your biology transforming from carbon base to crystalline base. Your immune system has worked by fighting invaders now the THYMUS absorbs and transmute invaders. All seven chakras are integrating so we have the one larger heart chakra. Your higher self changes the codes and the biology changes accordingly. The little human only needs to allow and NOTICE the changes. You have now merged 80% of the little human with your higher self and you are functioning as soul more than like the little human.

Level 7 carries **95 to 100% light** andis called **SOARING** the little human emotions, drama and concerns are mostly a thing of the past BUT your biology is still in the 4th dimension and needs to be lovingly cared for. The little human contribution is to be present in their biology awake and aware in present time. You are 90% melded with your soul. Before moving to level 8 you MARRY your higher self / SOUL.

Level 8 carries **ONENESS** and infinity the human functioning as one unit with the higher self or soul and you are out of duality spiritually, mentally and emotionally. Your biology is a vehicle from earth. The loneliness is gone now.

Level 9 is the **COMPLETION** of an era, a cycle, or level for you personally and it is not physical death or loss of your biology. It is the silence of completion.

286 humans on earth have reached level nine as of June 2010.

Chapter 7
The UNIVERSAL LAWS

The **LEGION OF LIGHT** is a term used to represent god or the creator or the source. Whatever name you use for the core of the creator and universal energy, which is unconditional love and compassion for all. The source is a partnership and not a singular entity. The legion of light ARE light-beings that are primarily consciousness and have no shape. Light-beings NEVER cease to exist but a soul can cease to exist, some follow the little human into darkness.

The legion of light is not in a place since the concept of "place" does not exist in a quantum state. Interdimensional energy is timeless and there is no place and no time on the other side of the veil. So there is no PAST and no FUTURE. There is only the now moment or present time in circles overlaying themselves.

The **UNIVERSAL LAWS** are the body of self-evident divine commandments generated from the legion of light's ONLY commandment "GIVE and RECEIVE only unconditional love and compassion" to keep the universe or cosmos balanced and harmonious. The universal law governs all PHENOMENA including science, ethics and philosophy. In our physical world of lower vibration, THINGS and THOUGHTS are temporary. Working within the laws you are assured of positive outcomes eventually. The laws are all interrelated.

Understand that everything in the universe is energy including humans.

Going against the laws creates suffering to strongly point out a better direction. Your IGNORANCE or disregard of universal law invites serious censure and doubt from your higher self. The higher angelic realms do not judge breaking human law.

All living things with awareness and knowledge of the laws have the VITALITY and STRENGTH to gather what they need to grow and develop out of their dark confusion. The inner character you have shows in your growth or DECAY that develops during your challenging struggles with matter and duality.External results of an action are not significant.

The universal law of **ACTION** means you must ACT first in order for something you want to start moving in the direction you want it to move. Then your invisible aspects will co-create the action with you and others join in after you make the first move or many little moves to get things rolling and prove your commitment.

The universal law of **ALLOWING** means dropping ALL judgment, blame and emotional attachment to what others DO, SAY or think. They are on their own spiritual path with their invisible aspects. Allowing requires granting others, even children the right to BE just as they are doing whatever THEY choose. With higher vibrational thought, truths and self-love we evolve out of the circle of darkness, force and control. TOLERANCE is not allowing it is holding negative thoughts.

The universal law of **ATTRACTION** says the thoughts and emotions of the little human create a vibrational energy consciously or unconsciously that emanates from us and attracts like energy. The universe does not care if your emanations are real or IMAGINED, negative or positive. It simply reflects with CLARITY and TRUTH what is held in your energy field. Moving to the larger realities and truths enable us to release our rage, anger and frustration. The human is a temporary vehicle and was never designed to RULE we are here to experience.

The universal law of **BALANCE** is to maintain order and harmony within the divine universe. Accept and OWN the human traits you have in the now moment. Accept and own the things and awareness your invisible aspects present to you. Each entity makes the CHOICE to exist. When those choices are made in synchronicity with the flow of other entities and EVENTS balance is maintained. Humans are 10% of their soul and we are balancing spiritual energy with physical matter. For every action there is a reaction. You may not know what the reaction is but there is one some place. Nothing happens the way you expect it to. BUT you NEED to notice it when it does happen and take advantage of their expert help.

The universal law of **CAUSE and EFFECT or RECIPROCAL action** is that nothing happens by CHANCE or outside of universal laws. Every action has a reaction or consequence. You get back what you give ALL the TIME so be conscious of your emanations. IT IS NOT personal it is physics. Keep functioning at a survival level and you will keep attracting survival situations to master for your spiritual awareness on that level.

The universal law of **CORRESPONDENCE** is "As above, so below." The laws of physics explaining the physical world of energy, light, vibration, and motion have their corresponding principles in the etheric world.

The universal law of **DIVINE MANIFESTATION** is win-win-win-win to benefit all involved and harm done to none. Any harm to another in the process or outcome of manifestation is not DIVINE and carries karmic debt.

The universal law of **ENTRAINMENT** REQUIRES that two resonances or vibrations existing in the same location MUST adjust and combine to have a single resonance. For Example, on a scale of 1-10 if one individual is at 3 and the other is at a 7 the law of entrainment requires that they will both be at 5 ish. The other possibility is when one resonance is overpowering it will pull the other to their level so you both would move to 3,4 or 6,7. Every thought we have creates energetic ripples. Our body anchors our energetic layers, which fan out in every direction in ever-widening circles of vibrating frequency at six feet from the biology. PRINCIPLE of Reconciliation and / or entrainment allows different qualities to get unified into similarities to diminish differences and decrease conflict and promote commonalities and oneness.

The universal law of **FREE WILL** is divine will granting each entity the right to DIRECT and PURSUE his or her life so long as he or she does not violate the same right of others. A right that excludes the rights of others is NOT DIVINE.

The universal law of **LOVE or DIVINE ONENESS** is everything is created from universal energy or unconditional love. All entities acceptWHAT IS. Free will does not come in PORTIONS you either have it or you do not have it. The Universe is a place of creation, experience and connection to everything else.

The universal law of **MACROCOSM and MICRO-COSM** is the first law of infinity. The whole of a complex structure is represented more or less in all of its parts, depending on the ordering of those parts. A drop of water has what the ocean has.

The universal law of **PERPETUAL TRANSMUTA-TION of ENERGY** is that all humans have the power to change the conditions in their lives. Raising your vibration IS HARD work. You need to stay in your biology and focus your thoughts. We ALL have the skill set to do that. What you have attracted you have to UNDO yourself.

The **PRINCIPLES** are derived from the universal laws and fundamental truths, found within the laws. A principle is a MORALLY correct behavior and attitude or a general scientific theorem or law having many special applications across a wide field. EXTERNAL results of an action are not significant. It is the inner CHARACTER growth or DECAY that develops during a challenging struggle in your experience that matters and reflects your vibration.

The principle of **ACTUALITY** is a thought or belief does not need to exist in material or dimensional form.

The principle of **AUTHORITY** is the one who is aware and capable of accepting the responsibility for an act and is WORTHY of having the authority to act will initiate and accept the responsibility for the act. Many want authority and they will not accept responsibility for and wish to avoid the consequence of their actions. It is either / or.

The principle of **AWARENESS** is when you observe the ILLUSION of separation but do not get CONFUSED or caught in the illusion or matrix. Earth is a role playing game designed to increase your wisdom and discernment.

The principle of **COMPENSATION** is what we think, speak and act we receive in the same kind or energy. Not in the exact manner and time we choose. Our invisible aspects set up synchronicities and rewards in there own way. No service lovingly and willingly given goes unrewarded. The reward is as large as you are able to RECEIVE. You need to NOTICE the reward and be a gracious receiver of what you do receive. We create limitation through refusal to see, own and use what we have been lovingly given.

The principle of **ENTHUSIASM** is discovering NEW things about the self and your thoughts or beliefs that make you feel enthusiastic about your existence. Continually a new belief shows up to CHALLENGE your old belief. The old belief crashes and you develop new higher vibrational truths. Each time we do this we get a little closer to our soul or invisible aspects. This repeated action INCREASES our enthusiasm.

Stagnating in old patterns makes us become robotic with lost enthusiasm for life and we STOP progressing. The lack of personal and spiritual growth depletes our energy because we have cut the connection to our higher self, becoming robotic clones.

The principle of **EXPANSION or INCLUSION** is never-ending as long as there is more to be included in the definition or description. We are all that THERE IS and all that can possibly be. When you move form expansion to EXCLUSION or contraction you describe something LESS than all that is, and that limits you. Describing the self as being this, but not that is limiting you.

The principle of **FREEDOM** is to give space for expansion and growth for ALL without restricting others freedom and space to grow. Universal law frees each and everyone. No one is free until each is free and all are freeing each other.

The principle of **GRACE**states that any Divine Being can apply the LAW OF MERCY and set aside karma.

The principle of **HAPPINESS** is how you FEEL about WHO you are, what you do, and what you have that creates happiness. Not who you are, what you do, or HAVE.

The principle of **HARMONY and AGREEMENT** says efforts to manipulate, trick, coerce or force harmony and agreement will only DISRUPT previously established areas of harmony and agreement. Between the most hostile enemies the smallest area of harmony and agreement can be discovered and increased.

The principle of **INERTIA** a body at rest remains at rest until an equal and opposite reaction happens moving the body at rest into another dimension or vibration like an echoing effect of an action.

The principle of **JOY and INNER PEACE** increases with each deeper connection of the little human and their invisible aspects. This process of surrender and allowing and giving up human free will for living in divine will.

The principle of **LEVERAGE** is a small amount of energy exerted in present time is used to change the course of future events. A change in consciousness NOW will change future experiences. The future or past is never fixed in multidimensions.

The principle of **LIABILITY** says WE ARE held liable for the use or ABUSE of whatever rights we have. For using or neglecting to use the rights we earned and have.

The principle of **MONEY** is an artificially created symbol used as a substitute for stored or BORROWED energies, that are EARNED, spent, OWED, claimed or exchanged. To be GOOD the symbol must be acceptable to others in a society who is willing to part with valuables or energies in exchange for the money symbol.

The principle of **PARADOX** recognizes the movement of energies in four dimensions simultaneously. Paradox combines Cause and Effect, Inertia, Microcosm and Macrocosm and Vibration. Energies do come together in a collision at a certain point. Paradox seen on a flat plane is like a stone dropped in a stream with the ripples moving out. Paradox in a CUBED space would create VIBRATIONS in all directions. Paradox touches into high levels of vibration and dense levels of vibration SIMUTANIOUSLY that the entire area appears to be alive. Whatever is said about one level can hold true for the next level and can also appear to be untrue.

The principle of **PEACE** comes from the human peaceful surrender to the soul. If the surrender is hostile or angry GREAT conflict will follow. ANY compromise with a force, divides, oppresses or harms INSTEAD of unifies. Harmony may be found IN CONFLICT when that is essential for the welfare of everyone involved. INNER peace nourishes external harmony and increments as yes and no merge into a MAYBE.

The principle of **PENETRATION** is anything that is seen with great attention and quality of awareness penetrates the heart, which emanates into all of consciousness.

The principle of **POVERTY** is to the degree you WITHHOLD your productivity and energy in hope that someone else will offer his or her energy instead, you EARN and experience poverty.

Poverty comes when you are productive and FAIL to properly take hold and claim your reward in a suitable manner.

Poverty comes to those who attempt to unfairly claim the energies of another or squander their blessings.

Poverty comes to those fixated on pinching pennies because they lose friends, health and opportunities.

Poverty comes to those filling their life with excessive TRASH or hoard.

Poverty comes to those who FOCUS on ONE thing at any cost.

Those convinced that they are unworthy or incapable of having anything of value will be in poverty. Outer benefits will bring little or no happiness or relief. Joy and wealth must be generated from attitudes and thoughts WITHIN you.

The principle of **PRIVACY** is every person is entitled to privacy we can't infringe on this right of individual privacy. No mind reading or questioning their motives or thoughts concerning there personal lives without consent.

The principle of **PROJECTION** is that the story of one's life and concurrent lives are stored within you and can only be changed or rewritten from within you by changing your thoughts. The intimate conversations, beliefs and relationship one has are reflected in experiences on the outer screen of life. We are both the camera and projector of our own life story.Those wishing to see joyous experiences instead of reruns, trash films, soap operas, tragedies, illness and hostilities, must refuse to bring or allow such films, concepts or images to fill their storage banks and consciousness.

The principle of **PROSPERITY** you prosper in direct proportion to the enjoyment you receive in seeing the prosperity of yourself and others. Your prosperity is denied in direct proportion to your feeling GUILT, envy or HOSTILITY for being prosperous or witnessing other's prosperity. When one prospers all may prosper. Those who think, feel, act and speak of themselves as being poor and needy must spend three times the energy for the same prosperity received by those who think, feel, act, and speak of themselves as being wealthy and prosperous. An attitude of depression leads to the way of physical, spiritual, mental, social and financial depression. Maintain a prosperous attitude even in states of poverty to move to those prosperous states.

The principle of **REALITY** is a measurable thing like an idea, object, event or person that can be seen, heard, felt, and then this object has reality or mass.

The principle of **RELATIVITY** is viewing everything and understanding all things from a particular viewpoint. With a desire for greater awareness comes knowledge of higher truths. EACH viewpoint is relative to the viewer's point of perception and is accurate for them. Each person receives a series of problems to strengthen their awareness and understanding of the next level of truths. Consider each test a challenge and remain connected to your heart. Put everything into its proper perspective.

The principle of **RESPONSIBILITY** is when you have the ability to respond to the needs of others you receive energy from all those you respond to. This is not stealing energy but creating energy together synergistically.

The principle of **SECURITY** you can express in a manner that allows your best performance without infringing on the expression of others that have the same right.

The principle of **SILENCE** when the little human views experiences THROUGH the souls point of perception and feeling you can experience even chaos from a level of nonresistant and silence.

The principle of **THOUGHT** is energy follows your THOUGHT. Seek information and your thought takes you there so you can discern what you want on that subject.

The principle of **the UNCONSCIOUS MIND / BRAIN** is that it is unable to distinguish FACT from FICTION. It follows what it is told. If convinced a piece of ice is red hot it will experience a burn.If convinced you are a failure it will make sure that you fail. If it receives conflicting data it produces conflicting results.

The principle of**VIBRATION** everything in the Universe, physical or not moves in waves or circular patterns and vibrates. That applies to our sensory perceptions, thoughts and all else has its own vibrational frequency, color and sound unique to itself.

꤇

CONCEPTS to INCORPORATE

Below are concepts to incorporate and always work on. The order you choose to master these in does not matter.

1. Relate to all others without BLAME, judgment or DRAMA.
2. Knowing comes first and then there is action or creating.
3. Connect to yourself and stand in your belief's loud and proud.
4. Fall into harmony with your soul and invisible aspects.
5. Align with the cosmic order and the way of things.
6. Align with the legion of light know and honor that.
7. Know the little human is experiencing duality on behalf its soul.
8. Consciously allow the order and flow of the universe.
9. TRUST yourself and what you know.
10. LOVE yourself unconditionally first.
11. Compassion and Love for SELF first and then ALL else.
12. Creating or manifesting is what we DO.

ABOUT YOU

Your entourage or more accurately your invisible aspects hold your entire story along with everyone else's story and they are happy to share it WHEN you are ready to hear it. Just ask them. They are waiting for you to find them inside of you and commune with them.

The FULL knowledge of what actually happened to you and your reaction to what happened will heal your programming, addictions and the self-destructive patterns you hold dear. Putting a pretty story on your childhood experiences and concurrent lives to please or deny will not change a thing and it never has.

About Me

I have been an educational therapist for the past few decades and have done private therapy with children, adults and families. I understand how devastating CHILD abuse is and how it will negatively impact a person of any age. For the past 40 years I have taught emotionally challenged and severely learning disabled students and adults from grades 3-12 in public schools as well as in my own private school, these experiences have showed me what works and what does not work so well.

The "cause and effect" of things have always fascinated me and I always want to "know more" so I studied the field of psychology and sociology my entire existence and many more lifetimes than just this one. The illuminati programmed have showed up at my door and I wanted to help them.

Inside you KNOW

Bonnie

CERTIFICATIONS

Educational Therapist, National

Principal and Reading specialist K-12 Arizona

Emotionally and Learning Disabled K-12 Arizona and Texas

Art Instructor and Supervisor K-14 Illinois

EDUCATION

University of Phoenix

National College of Education (now National-Louis University) Major: Special Education

North Park College—Chicago, Illinois

EXPERIENCE

Acting Principal, Program Director and Community Coordinator for the Severely Emotionally Disabled, grades 7-12. Designed, developed and implemented a therapeutic approach. Collaborated with psychologists, peace officers, parents and Administrators. Have designed, developed and implemented curriculum, for at-risk, multicultural students in inner cities. Facilitated group processing. Helped to transition students into the mainstream, Student advocate for student's and families rights. Peace Officer for Harris County, Texas. Member of the Biltmore Who's Who. I have worked with many illuminati slaves to crash their programs.

www.ingramcontent.com/pod-product-compliance
Lightning Source LLC
Chambersburg PA
CBHW072134280526
45788CB00002B/627